Kindergarten Teacher's Guide

EVERY DAY COUNTS®

CALENDAR MATH

Beth Ardell

Janet G. Gillespie

Patsy F. Kanter

GReaT SoURCe®

EDUCATION GROUP

A Houghton Mifflin Company

New Ways to Know®

ACKNOWLEDGMENTS

We offer special thanks to

- **our mentors:** the late Mary Baratta-Lorton, Marilyn Burns, Andy Clark, Patricia Davidson, Constance Kamii, Kathy Pfaendler, Kathy Richardson, Allyn Snider, and the late Robert Wirtz for inspiring and guiding our work in the classroom through their workshops and writing.
- **our families:** Tom, Benjamin, Nicholas, Caitlin, and Matthew Ardell; Tim, Nathan, and Josh Gillespie; and David, Julie, and Nathan Kanter for their wisdom, understanding and loving support.
- **the Great Source team:** Evelyn Curley, Betsy Donaghey, Rick Duthe, Kathy Kellman, Susan Rogalski, and Richard Spencer, for making this edition of *Every Day Counts® Calendar Math* a reality.

CREDITS

Cover design: Kristen Davis, Great Source
Cover art: Amy Vangsgard & Kristen Davis
Design: Taurins Design
Electronic art: Taurins Design

Printed in China

Great Source®, *Every Day Counts®*, and *New Ways to Know®* are registered trademarks of Houghton Mifflin Company.

International Standard Book Number-10: 0-669-51436-5

International Standard Book Number-13: 978-0-669-51436-0

6 7 8 9 10 - RRDS - 09 08 07

TABLE OF CONTENTS

Dear Fellow Teachers,

We are so glad that you have chosen *Every Day Counts® Calendar Math* for your classroom. For our new users, welcome and for our veteran users, thanks for your continued confidence in and support for *Every Day Counts Calendar Math*.

Every Day Counts Calendar Math is built on our many years of classroom experience teaching mathematics. An interactive K-6 supplemental mathematics program, *Every Day Counts Calendar Math* is designed to capitalize on daily discussions to foster children's mathematical confidence and competence. The program is based on our observations from our years of teaching and is supported by research that shows:

1. Children need to learn mathematics incrementally, giving them the opportunity to develop understandings over time.

2. Visual models help children visualize and verbalize number and geometric relationships.

3. Classroom discussion fosters the growth of language acquisition and development of reasoning. It also allows children to discover that there are many strategies for solving problems.

4. Over time, children can learn to think algebraically. Early exposure to this type of thinking will lead them to a successful future in mathematics.

5. Observing and listening to children is essential to ongoing assessment that can guide instruction.

This edition of *Every Day Counts Calendar Math* has new features to reduce your workload, and new elements to increase the level of success for your students. The Teacher's Guide is organized to aid instruction: **Concepts and Skills** tell the focus of each lesson, **Author Notes** explain the thinking behind the elements, **Materials** and **Setup** list preparation tips, and **Daily Routine** outlines the update procedure. As always **Discussion** offers questions and sample dialogues to help guide your lessons, and **Helpful Hints** further enrich the lessons. New to this edition are **Ongoing Assessment** questions that reveal individual children's knowledge and help you to meet different students' instructional needs. Ongoing Assessment also appears in a separate booklet in the kit for easy use during Calendar time.

The kit contains the usual materials needed to get started—counting tape paper, a Calendar, Calendar Pieces for each month, month strips, yesterday, today, and tomorrow markers for grades K–2, demo coins, play money for grades 3–5, and plastic pockets. New to this kit are some background posters to arrange the bulletin board with ease, Counting Tape Pieces to count the days in school, manipulatives, paper clips to get the calendars ready for immediate use, and storage bags.

We have learned much from our teaching colleagues and appreciate their support, suggestions and the opportunities to teach together. Most of all we offer our thanks to our main teachers—the children throughout the country with whom we've had the privilege to work, and who have taught us so much. Best wishes to you as you teach math this year and in years to come.

Collegially,

Beth Ardell   *Janet Gillespie*   *Patsy F. Kanter*

WELCOME TO EDC CALENDAR MATH

Every Day Counts® Calendar Math appeals to the natural way children learn math—building on concepts a little at a time, every day. Simple to use, the Teacher's Guide and kit contain a full year of activities with suggestions for discussions that will have your students excited about "talking math."

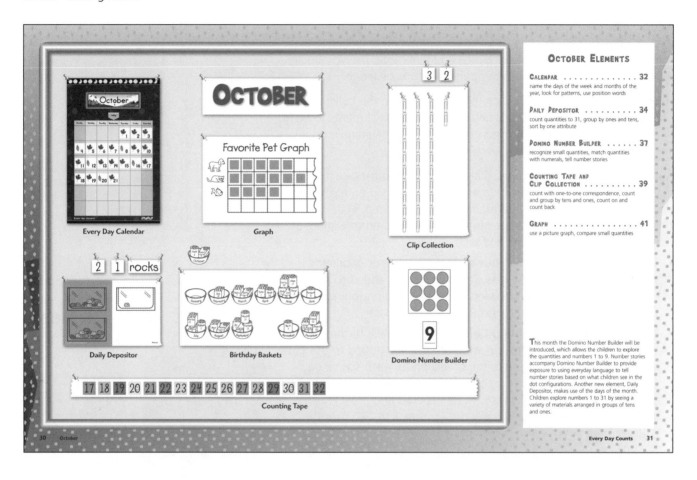

OCTOBER ELEMENTS

This month the Domino Number Builder will be introduced, which allows the children to explore the quantities and numbers 1 to 9. Number stories accompany Domino Number Builder to provide exposure to using everyday language to tell number stories based on what children see in the dot configurations. Another new element, Daily Depositor, makes use of the days of the month. Children explore numbers 1 to 31 by seeing a variety of materials arranged in groups of tens and ones.

Every Day Calendar · Graph · Clip Collection · Daily Depositor · Birthday Baskets · Domino Number Builder · Counting Tape

A lot of math in a little time. In just 10–15 minutes a day, *Every Day Counts* provides supplemental math instruction that revolves around a simple interactive bulletin board with a variety of elements, or components. As children build the bulletin board, they also build mathematical understanding and confidence. Great progress is made in small incremental steps.

Children learn from their discoveries. Students' observations and thinking are the driving force behind *Every Day Counts.* Different monthly elements provide a continuous learning experience in which students examine mathematical relationships central to the curriculum for their grade level. This daily, visual, hands-on exposure to critical math concepts complements the natural way children learn—building on concepts a little at a time, every day, to help them develop mathematical competence and confidence.

"The EDC board was a hit with my kids because it was interactive and it was not from a book. It was almost difficult to convince them that it was math! It dovetailed into so many areas that the book covers anyway, it was either a great introduction or a great review for many concepts."

Linda Hoerling-Glenn
Teacher, Tacoma, WA

Classroom discussion: the heart of *Every Day Counts*. With the discussion questions that are provided for a variety of levels, children use mathematical language to explain their thinking in the common "folk language" of math such as "I had 5 marbles and I got 3 more, and now I have 8." Asking students to share the various ways they arrived at answers helps them see that

- There are many ways to work with numbers
- There is more than one way to approach a problem
- The same way of working out a problem may be explained in several different ways.

As Calendar Math conversations continue and grow in depth throughout the year, children begin to use formal math language in context and with increasing confidence and familiarity. The vocabulary makes sense to them and becomes part of their knowledge.

Help for struggling learners. Incremental changes in the bulletin board allow English Language Learners and struggling math students to build skills and understanding at a comfortable rate. If understanding does not come immediately, there is always another day.

A mathematical kaleidoscope. With *Every Day Counts,* each day is slightly different from the day before. As students build on each of the elements, new relationships are examined and discussed. In kindergarten the following elements encourage children to explore a year's worth of math concepts and skills:

- **The Calendar** presents a unique pattern of colors or geometric shapes each month as one new Calendar Piece is added to the display each day. Children develop patterning and reasoning skills as they try to predict what the next Piece will look like.
- **The Counting Tape and Clip Collection** keep track of the number of days of school as one new numbered square is added to the Tape and one paper clip is added to the collection for each school day. Children see counting patterns and develop number sense as the sequence of numbers progresses from 1 to 180 and the accompanying clip quantity slowly grows from 1 to 180 over the course of the entire year.
- **Domino Number Builder** activities vary slightly from month to month as children color dots on giant Dominos to develop instant recognition of small sets, match them to numerals, and see how small sets combine.
- **Daily Depositor** builds a variety of collections that increase by one each day of the month, exposing children to place value concepts using the numbers 1 to 31.
- **Estimation and Measurement** helps children experience the language of estimation, comparing and measuring as they keep track of nonstandard units such as scoops of rice or connecting cubes accumulating a day at a time.
- **Graph** offers children the opportunity to collect, graph, and analyze a variety of data such as class birthday dates, weather records, and the results of favorite pet polls.

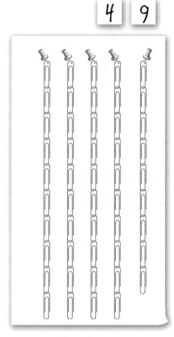

Clip Collection

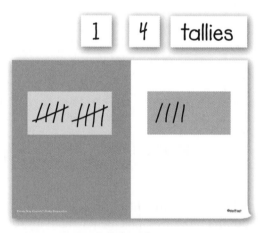

Daily Depositor

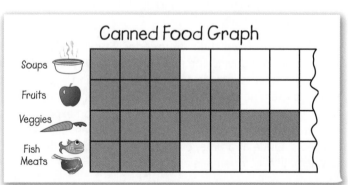

Graph

A Comprehensive Teacher's Guide. The Teacher's Guide for each grade level of *Every Day Counts* is organized by month and by elements. Each month begins with a picture of what the bulletin board might look like toward the middle of the month. A brief overview of suggested elements and activities for the month follows. As each element is introduced, you will find:

- **Concepts & Skills** for that activity
- A list of **Materials** for the activities, all either in the kit or readily available like paper clips
- The **Daily Routine** provides an easy-to-follow explanation of how to present this month's activities
- **Discussions** offer suggestions for discussion and assessment as well as sample dialogues
- **Helpful Hints** to share ideas such as games, literature, or extensions of the month's activities. Many of these hints originated with teachers using *Calendar Math* in their classrooms.

Key math **vocabulary** terms are highlighted where they are first introduced and are also illustrated in the Teacher Resource section.

ONGOING ASSESSMENT TOOLS

- The **Ongoing Assessment** booklet provides an organized list of suggested assessment questions for use with each month's activities. These questions may also be used as a quick reference guide to instruction on days that time is limited.
- Each month **Ongoing Assessment** questions for each element are provided in the Teacher's Guide to help you gain insight into children's developing mathematical thinking.
- The teacher's everyday role is that of observer, listener, recorder, and questioner. Through daily observations and listening to children's discussions, assessment is ongoing.
- Assessment copy masters in the Teacher's Guide provide an easy way to capture progress at significant points of the year. A pretest for the beginning of the year allows you to assess children's prior knowledge. Two interim tests and a post test for the end of the year help you to gauge growth of understanding.

Every Day Counts® Calendar Math **is supported by research and practice.** Research shows that continuous exposure to critical math concepts allows children to develop an understanding of important mathematical concepts over time and to learn at an individual pace. Experience from classroom practice demonstrates that young children actively, incrementally construct mathematical knowledge. Understanding is solidified through reflection on real-life data, group discussion, and cooperative problem solving. The topics and challenges at each grade are aligned with NCTM standards and build on what students learn in class with activities that engage students, allowing them to explore, make and test conjectures, and apply their mathematics. Students using *Every Day Counts® Calendar Math* have been shown to develop higher-level thinking skills, enjoy math more, see its application in the real world, and score higher on standardized tests.

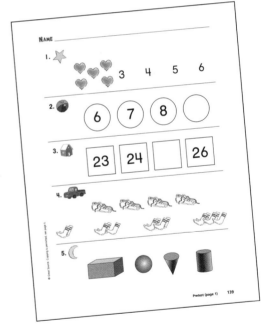

There is little preparation for *Every Day Counts Calendar Math.* Once the materials are prepared and organized, your prep work for the year is minimal.

The following materials will be very useful in organizing and preparing the materials in your kit: a roll of masking tape; a craft knife; a box of bulletin board push pins; a sheet of 12" × 18" construction paper.

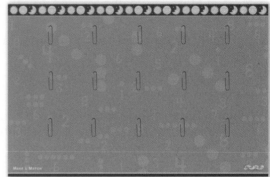

Make a Match poster

Preparing the Posters

Many teachers have found that a "slit and clip" method works best to attach the Calendar Pieces and other kit items to the Calendar, Daily Depositor, and Make a Match posters. To prepare the Calendar use a craft knife to place a half-inch cut at the top of each space on the Calendar. You'll find a hairline rule at the top of each space to show you where to make the slit. Insert a small paper clip in each slit. Each Calendar Piece will slide beneath a clip. This "slit-and-clip" method makes it easy for both you and the children to put the pieces on and take them off for counting. It also allows you to place the Calendar on a wall or other surface that doesn't accept push pins. To secure the paper clips, put strips of masking tape over the paper clips on the back of the Calendar. Use the same technique on the Daily Depositor and Make a Match posters.

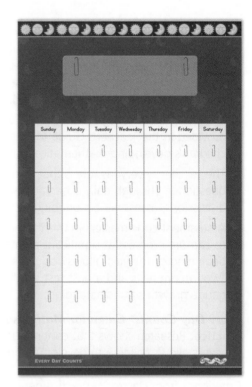

Calendar

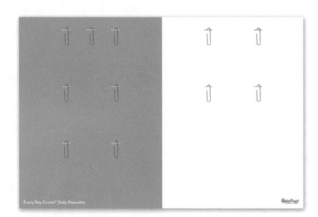

Daily Depositor

Preparing the Counting Tape and Clip Collection

Use the roll of adding machine tape in the kit to create the base of the Counting Tape. Cut a piece of adding machine tape 4–5 feet long and attach it to the wall above your bulletin board. You will use the colored paper squares included in the kit to build the Counting Tape throughout the school year. To make the Counting Tape continuous, add additional sections of adding machine tape as needed throughout the year. A plain sheet of 12" x 18" paper provides the background to pin the Clip Collection onto.

ORGANIZING THE CARDSTOCK

You have a set of cardstock Calendar Pieces for the Calendar that are organized and labeled by month. Carefully punch out a set (three sheets) for each month. Put each month's pieces in the resealable plastic bags and label them with the name of the month. Punch out and attach the Today Arrow Marker to the Calendar and store it with your first month's Calendar Pieces.

CHOOSING AMONG THE POSSIBILITIES

Flip to the beginning of each month in this Teacher's Guide and scan through the range of elements that make up *Every Day Counts* at your grade level. The first year you might want to start small and limit the number of elements you share with the class. Your preparation can be minimized, and your primary focus can be facilitating class discussions. Begin with the year-long elements–the Counting Tape and Clip Collection and the Calendar. You might also choose an element that provides experience with a topic students have had difficulty with in the past. As the year goes by and you become familiar with the program, you may choose to add new elements to further enrich your discussions.

ARRANGING THE EDC BULLETIN BOARD DISPLAY

Choose a place in your room where you can create a bulletin board that is easily accessible to you and your students. Many teachers who use *Every Day Counts* do not hang everything in one location. Sometimes Graphs are placed across the room or the Counting Tape is hung under the chalkboard. Some teachers choose an area where children can gather together on the floor to hold daily class meetings to make updates to the bulletin board.

PLANNING CLASS TIME

We recommend that the EDC discussion last for only 10–15 minutes each day. In order to stay within this time period all displays are updated, but only 1–2 elements are discussed. A quick update of the Counting Tape in Grade 3 might flow like this:

Teacher: Yesterday we had been in school 47 days. How many days have we been in school as of today?

Class: 48.

Teacher: Will today's square be pink or yellow?

Class: Yellow because 48 is an even number.

This simple update takes less than 30 seconds. If the Counting Tape is to be discussed, an extended series of questions might be asked, such as:

- What day will it be in three days?
- How did you figure out that answer?
- Talk to us about a pattern you see on the Counting Tape.

If a special occasion means you will not have time for any EDC discussion, at least commit to keeping the display updated so the elements are always current.

Every classroom runs on a different schedule. You may have special events, field trips, or snow days that change your daily routine. To help you keep track of the concepts you want to cover with *Every Day Counts Calendar Math,* we have provided a simple planner copy master that you can use to organize your plans.

EDC WEEKLY PLANNER

	MONDAY Date: Nov 16 Day in School: 47	TUESDAY Date: Nov 17 Day in School: 48	WEDNESDAY Date: Nov 18 Day in School: 49	THURSDAY Date: Nov 19 Day in School: 50	FRIDAY Date: Nov 20 Day in School: 51
Materials to Prepare	None		Graph Temp: a cold day! colder, coldest? C Tape how many to 50?	Measurement How Many Steps? C Tape a Big Day!	Calendar notice diagonals Depositor 2 groups of 10
Element to Discuss	Calendar when will we get the next square? Domino Guess my Domino: 1 more, 1 less	Depositor how many more to fill grid? C Tape how many more to 50?			
Concepts to Focus on	Predicting, 1 more, 1 less	Counting on, how many more?	How many more, 1 more	Half, estimating	Groups of 10
Children to Observe	Carmen – let her find tomorrow	Carmen again	Tia, Yoko – 1 more?	Julie – hear her ideas about 50 and 100	Mark, Josh – do they see the tens?
Special Days				Halfway to 100!	

Every Day Counts

11

EDC Weekly Planner

	MONDAY Date: _____ Day in School: _____	TUESDAY Date: _____ Day in School: _____	WEDNESDAY Date: _____ Day in School: _____	THURSDAY Date: _____ Day in School: _____	FRIDAY Date: _____ Day in School: _____
Materials to Prepare					
Element to Discuss					
Concepts to Focus on					
Children to Observe					
Special Days					

Numbers & Operations	Aug/Sept	Oct	Nov	Dec	Jan	Feb	Mar	April	May/June
compose & decompose numbers	CT	D, CT DO	CT, D,	CT, D, DO	CT, D, DO	CC, CT, DO	C, CT, DO	CT, D, DO	CT, DO
use place value models	CT	CT, D	CT, D	CT, D	CT, D	C, CC, CT, D	C, CT, D	CT, D	CT, D
compare & order numbers	C, CT	C, CT, DO	C, CT	C, CT, DO	C, CT, DO	C, CT, G	C, CT	C, CT	C, CT
relate number words and numerals to quantities	C, CT	C, CT, D, DO	C, CT, D, DO	C, CT, D, DO	CT, D, DO	C, CT, D, DO	C, CT, D, DO	C, CT, D, DO	C, CT, D, DO, G
one-to-one correspondence	C, CT	CT, D, DO	C, CT, D, DO	C, D, DO	CT, D, DO	C, D, DO	CT, D, DO	C, CT, D, DO	C, CT, D, DO, G
understand ordinal numbers	G	C, CT	DO	C	DO	DO	DO		
read numerals	C, CT	C, CT, D	C, CT	C, CT, D	C, CT, D, DO	C, CT, D, DO	C, CT, D	C, CT, D	C, CT, D
write numerals	CT	DO	D	D	D	CT, D, DO	D	D, DO, M	D
use odd & even numbers						C, CT	DO	M	
addition concepts	G	CT, D	CT, D	CT, D, DO	CT, D, DO	C, CT, D, DO	C, CT, D, DO	CT, D, DO	CT, D, DO
subtraction concepts	G	CT	CT	CT, D	CT, G	CT	CT	CT	CT
equal groupings, equal shares (groupings of 10)	C, CT	CT, D	CT, D	CT, D	CT, D	CT, D	CT, D	CT, D	CT, D, DO
compare quantities	G	CT, D, DO, G	CT, DO, G	CT, DO, G	CT, D, G	CT, G	CT, G	CT, G, M	CT, G
fractions						C, CT		C	C
count objects to 100	G, C, CT	C, CT, D, DO, G	C, CT, D, DO, G	C, CT, D, DO, G	C, CT, D, DO, G	C, CT, D, DO, G	C, CT, D, DO, G	C, CT, D, DO, G	C, CT, D, DO, G
count objects over 100						CT	CT	CT	CT
count by 2, 5, or 10	CT	CT, D	CT, D	CT, D, DO, G	C, CT, D	C, CT, D	C, CT, D	CT, D	CT, D
counting on	C, CT	C, CT, D	C, CT	C, CT, D, DO	C, CT	C, CT	C, CT, G	C, CT, D	C, CT, D
counting back	CT	C, CT	C, CT	C, CT	C, CT	C, CT	C, CT, G	C, CT	C, CT
mental math	CT	CT, DO	C, CT	C, CT	C, CT	C, CT	C, CT	C, CT	C, CT

KEY

C = CALENDAR D = DAILY DEPOSITOR G = GRAPH
CT = COUNTING TAPE AND CLIP COLLECTION DO = DOMINO NUMBER BUILDER M = ESTIMATION AND MEASUREMENT

Patterns & Functions (Algebra)	Aug/Sept	Oct	Nov	Dec	Jan	Feb	Mar	April	May/June
patterns: sort, classify, and/or order objects	C, CT, G	C, CT, D	C, G	C	C, DO	C	C	C, M	C, CT
patterns: recognize, describe, and/or extend	C, CT	C, CT	C, CT, G	C, CT, D	C, CT, DO	C, CT	C, CT, DO, G	C, CT, DO, G	C, CT,
repeating patterns	C, CT	C, CT	C, CT	C, CT, D	C, CT	C, CT	C, CT	C, CT, M	CT
growing patterns									C
symbols: plus, minus, equals						DO	DO	DO	
model addition and subtraction w/objects		D	D	D	D, DO	D, DO	D, DO	D, DO	D, DO

KEY

C = CALENDAR D = DAILY DEPOSITOR G = GRAPH

CT = COUNTING TAPE AND CLIP COLLECTION DO = DOMINO NUMBER BUILDER M = ESTIMATION AND MEASUREMENT

Geometry & Measurement	Aug/Sept	Oct	Nov	Dec	Jan	Feb	Mar	April	May/June
properties of 2-D shapes	C		C	C	C		C	C	G
describe properties of 3-D shapes	G				C		C	C	G
spatial relationships: proximity, position, & direction		C, DO	C		DO	DO			C, CT, DO, G
relate geometry to measurement & number		DO	DO	C, DO	C, DO	DO			CT, D, G
geometric shapes in environment	G					C		C	G
length			M	D, M			M		
capacity/volume				D		M		M	
weight				G, M	M		M		
temperature words			G		G			G	
days of week	C	C, CT	C, D	C	C	C	C	C	C, CT
names of months	C, G	C	C	C	C	C	C	C	C
yesterday, today, tomorrow	C, CT	C, CT	C, CT, D	C, D ,CT	C ,CT	C, CT	C ,CT	C, CT	C, CT
explore time						C			
pennies						G	G	D	D
nickels							G		D
dimes								D	D
nonstandard units			M	M	M	M	M	M	M
measurement tools				M	M	M	M	M	M
compare and/or order objects by measurement			M	D, M	M	M	M	M	
common benchmarks							M		
compare measurements			M	M	M	M	M	M	
estimate measurements				G	M		M	M	

KEY

C = CALENDAR   D = DAILY DEPOSITOR   G = GRAPH
CT = COUNTING TAPE AND CLIP COLLECTION   DO = DOMINO NUMBER BUILDER   M = ESTIMATION AND MEASUREMENT

Data Analysis/Probability	Aug/Sept	Oct	Nov	Dec	Jan	Feb	Mar	April	May/June
gather data	G	G	G	G C,	G, M	G	G	G, M	G
organize and/or analyze data	G	D, G	G	G	G, M	G	G	G, M	C, CT, DO, G
bar graph		G	G	G	G	G	G	G	G
picture graph	G	G	G		G			G	G
scatter graphs	G				G				
tally charts					G	D			
sort and classify objects by attributes	C	D	G	G	DO				G
describe parts of data set and whole set	C, G	C, G	G	G	C, G	C, G	G	G	C, G
probability: likelihood and making predictions	C, G	CT, G	CT	D	C, G	C, G	C, G	C, M	C, CT

Problem Solving	Aug/Sept	Oct	Nov	Dec	Jan	Feb	Mar	April	May/June
apply a variety of appropriate strategies to solve problems (i.e. guess and check, work backward, make a list)	G		C, DO, G	D, DO	C, DO, G, M	C, DO	C, D, G	CT, D, DO, M	CT, DO
monitor and reflect on the process of mathematical problem solving		G, C		C, D, DO	C, DO, G, M	C, DO	C, DO, G	CT, D, DO, M	CT, DO

Reasoning & Proof	Aug/Sept	Oct	Nov	Dec	Jan	Feb	Mar	April	May/June
recognize reasoning and proof as fundamental aspects of mathematics	C	C, CT, G	C, CT	C, DO	C, G, M	C, CT, DO	C, G	CC, D, DO, G	C, CT, DO
select and use various types of reasoning and methods of proof	C, CT	CT, G	C, CT	C, G	C, G, M	C, DO	C, G	CC, D, DO, M	C, CT, DO

Communication, Connections & Representations	Aug/Sept	Oct	Nov	Dec	Jan	Feb	Mar	April	May/June
communicate mathematical thinking	C, DT, G	C, DO, G	C, CT, DO, G	C, D, DO, G, M	C, CT, D, DO, G, M	C, CT, D, DO	C, D, DO	C, CT, D, DO, G, M	C, CT, D, DO, G
recognize and use connections among mathematical ideas	C, G		G	C, DO, G	C, DO, G, M	C, DO	C, D	CT, D, DO	C, CT, DO, G
use representations to model and interpret mathematical phenomena	C, CT, G	C, CT, G	C	C, DO	C, DO, G	C, DO	C, G	DO, M	C, CT, DO, G

KEY

C = CALENDAR   D = DAILY DEPOSITOR   G = GRAPH

CT = COUNTING TAPE AND CLIP COLLECTION   DO = DOMINO NUMBER BUILDER   M = ESTIMATION AND MEASUREMENT

Every Day Calendar

Birthday Baskets

1 2 3 4 5 6 7 8 9 10 11 12

Counting Tape

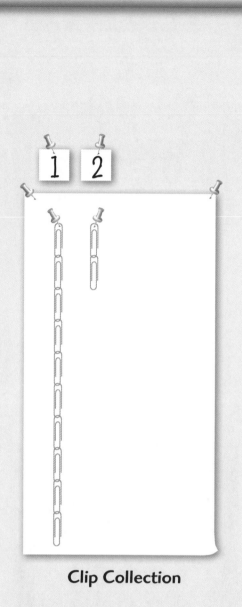

Clip Collection

Getting started in kindergarten requires only a few elements of Every Day Counts Calendar Math since establishing classroom routines and getting to know the children are your highest priorities.

If your school year begins in August, begin using the Counting Tape and Clip Collection during the first week; don't wait until September. To acknowledge August birthdays, introduce the Every Day Graph.

The Calendar pieces provided for August are a preview of the September pieces. You may want to allow children simply to observe the Calendar routine in August, and begin discussions in September. If, in September, kindergartners can begin to participate in group discussions and begin to develop the language for talking about the Calendar, then they will be able to engage in this activity in more depth in months to come.

Number & Operations   Algebra   Geometry   Measurement   Data & Probability
Problem Solving   Reasoning   Communication   Connections   Representation

CALENDAR

Concepts & Skills

- Know the days of the week in order
- Know the names of the months
- Count with one-to-one correspondence
- Read, compare, and order numbers 1 to 30
- Match quantities with numerals
- Analyze and extend patterns
- Develop number sense

Ongoing Assessment

1. What number do you see on today's Calendar Piece?

2. How many Calendar Pieces do we have on the Calendar today? How do you know?

3. Do we have more yellow circles or more green circles on the Calendar?

Materials for the Year

Every Day Calendar, Month Strip and Calendar Pieces for the current month, Today Arrow Marker, Calendar Record (TR2). Date Cards (TR1) or a non-permanent marker are needed for August and September.

Author Notes

"The Every Day Calendar provides more than a display of the days of the month. It uses special Calendar Pieces to create a specific pattern as they are displayed during the course of the month. Each month's pattern will be different. In September, the Calendar discussions will focus on the name of the current month, the order of the days of the week, the number of days in a week, and the identification of weekdays and weekend days. A weekday and weekend pattern (green for "go" days and yellow for "slow" days) is presented for the first month to help children relate the Calendar to their daily lives.

In the following months, other patterns are introduced, such as a simple sequence of alternating purple circles and red rectangles, or a repeated sequence of two yellow cylinders followed by one blue rectangular solid. By having the Calendar Pieces gradually reveal a pattern, the Calendar provides an invitation to find connections between the attributes of the pieces and the order in which they appear. Asking, "What will be the color on today's Calendar Piece?" encourages children to think about that connection. Later, children can make generalizations to predict the specific Piece that will appear on any future date using a variety of strategies."

Setup

- Post the Calendar in a place where children can comfortably gather around it.
- Before the first of the month, number the Calendar Pieces with a non-permanent marker. Alternatively, attach Date Cards from TR1 copied onto a transparency or paper and cut apart. Either way, you can reuse these Calendar Pieces in future years when weekday and weekend dates will differ.
- Store the Calendar Pieces in an envelope near the Calendar.

In September green circles are used for school days or weekdays, and yellow circles for weekend days. In August green and yellow squares showed the same pattern.

Daily Routine

- Begin with a blank Every Day Calendar. Post the current Month Strip on the Calendar and help the children read it aloud.
- Put up the Calendar Piece for the day. If the month began before the first day of school, catch up to the day's date with the class.
- Attach the Today Arrow Marker above the day's name in the top row, and read aloud the word *today*, as well as the day's name.
- Each school day, attach the day's new Calendar Piece. On Mondays, add the Calendar Pieces for Saturday and Sunday with the class before putting up Monday's piece.
- Each day as you put up the new Calendar Piece, move the Today Arrow Marker above the day's name and help the class read the date.
- Once a week in September discuss the emerging pattern with questions that draw attention to the weekday/weekend pattern.

DISCUSSION

For the Beginning of the Month

Pointing to the Calendar, read the name of each day of the week. Have children join you, making sure to chant one whole week before stopping on the current day. Toward the end of the first week, ask some of the following questions to encourage children to offer their own observations about the Calendar.

Number Sense To develop numeral recognition:

- What numbers do you see so far?
- What number do you think will be on tomorrow's piece?

Algebraic Thinking To look for similarities and differences:

- How are the pieces we've put up so far alike?
- How are they different?

If some children recognize the possibility of a repeating color pattern at this time, suggest that it may be fun to see if the colors keep coming up in this way. If a pattern is not mentioned, do not point one out at this time. The purpose of this early discussion is just to get children acquainted with the Calendar.

For the Middle of the Month

After a week or more, when several pieces are in view, begin asking the class each day to predict what color piece will appear. Allow volunteers to share how they came up with their predictions. Then reveal the day's piece and put it on the Calendar. On the 18th of the month, a classroom discussion similar to the one that follows might occur.

"What number do you think will be on tomorrow's piece?"

Days of the Week Song

Sunday, Monday, Tuesday, Wednesday, Thursday, Friday, Saturday! (repeat)

The days of the week can be sung to the tune of *Clementine*.

Sample Dialogue

Teacher: Let's look at the Calendar. What is today?

Class: Today is Friday, September 18th.

Teacher: What color will today's piece be?

Class: It will be green.

Teacher: What shape will it be?

Class: A circle.

Teacher: Let's look at today's piece. Yes, today's piece has an 18 on it and it is a green circle . Would someone like to tell us why it is green?

> Sample vocabulary words are also illustrated on TR27 and TR28. Encourage children to practice using these terms in class discussions.

Class: Today is a school day.

Teacher: Let's put it up on the Friday space. What day will it be tomorrow?

Class: Tomorrow will be Saturday, September 19th.

Teacher: Yes. What color do you think tomorrow's piece will be?

Child: It will be yellow.

Teacher: Who thinks it will be yellow? Who thinks it might be a different color? Can anyone find another Saturday and tell us its color?

Child: There's one above. It is yellow.

Teacher: Yes, that's right. You saw that Saturdays are yellow. When you see something happening over and over again, it is called a pattern. Patterns can help you guess what will happen next. Let's look at tomorrow's piece. Do you see anything else happening over and over again?

Below are some more questions to ask about weeks, weekends, and weekdays that will help you make the most of this month's Calendar and get children thinking.

Number Sense, Days of the Week To develop counting with one-to-one correspondence and familiarity with the weekdays:

- Would someone be willing to come up to the Calendar and point to all the days in one week?
- Can anyone help us count the number of days in one week?
- Would someone be willing to point out the weekdays, or school days, on the Calendar?
- What color are the weekdays on the Calendar?
- Can someone help us count the number of weekdays in one week?
- Can anyone show us another week with five weekdays and count them?
- Can anyone point out the weekend days on the Calendar?
- What color are weekend days?
- Would someone be willing to count the number of weekend days in one week?
- On which day of the week do we return to school after a weekend?
- In how many days will it be Monday?
- Can someone show how you figured that out?

"What color do you think tomorrow's piece will be?"

To Sum Up

At month's end, have children study the Calendar and ask them to share what they see happening on it. Their observations might include the following:

- There are more greens than yellows.
- The greens are always in the middle.
- I see yellow, green, green, green, green, green, yellow. It keeps happening over and over.

You might want to record student observations on a large poster that includes a smaller version of the Calendar. You can use the Calendar Record (TR2) for this purpose.

HELPFUL HINTS

- Some teachers prefer to make the Calendar Pieces match the seasons. For example, they might choose schoolhouses and school buses for September. Keep the pieces simple so the children can see the numbers clearly.
- You may want to hang a small commercial calendar next to the Every Day Calendar to help children to make connections with the real world.

Completed September Calendar

Number & Operations	Algebra	Geometry	Measurement	Data & Probability
Problem Solving	Reasoning	Communication	Connections	Representation

COUNTING TAPE

Concepts & Skills

- Develop number sense
- Count with one-to-one correspondence
- Match quantities with numerals
- Compare and order quantities
- Count on and count back
- Discover number patterns and use mental math
- Solve problems

Ongoing Assessment

1. What day of school came just after Day 9?
2. How are the squares that come after 10 different from the first 10? How are they alike?
3. How many days have we come to school since the 10th day?

Materials for the Year

Adding-machine tape, 20 three-inch squares in each of 10 different colors (200 total), 20 white $\frac{3}{4}$ inch dot stickers (optional), a bold black marker

Counting Tape on Day 16

Author Notes

"The Counting Tape is a time line for recording each day of kindergarten. As children see a new square added to the Counting Tape each day and see the number for that school day recorded, they will become familiar with increasing quantities and the numbers that represent them.

The color changes each day, and the repetition of the color sequence in each decade transforms the Counting Tape into a pattern that highlights the pattern of our counting system. As children count the squares each day, they practice the counting sequence. Then every ten days children see the pattern, 1 to 9 followed by a new ten, repeated. Beginning in November, two hands showing 10 fingers will be hung under each multiple of ten on the Counting Tape. Asking questions such as, "What day of school will it be in 2 more school days?" will help children develop language that describes the passage of time and gain skills in counting on.

The Counting Tape reveals other relationships as well. Its linearity makes it easy to see which is more, 12 or 21. Making such comparisons fosters children's development of number sense."

Setup

Display a 4- or 5-foot length of adding machine tape prominently in the room. Add additional segments as needed throughout the year.

Daily Routine

- Beginning on the first day of school, attach one square to the adding-machine tape each day.

- Use ten different-colored squares for the first ten days, then repeat the same sequence of colors for the remaining days of school.

- Each day in September ask the class to count by ones to the day's square. Record the number on the square.

- After Day 10, also count by tens and ones, clapping on the last multiple of ten as a reminder to change the counting pattern and begin counting by ones. For example, on the 14th day of school, children count, "10 (with a clap), 11, 12, 13, 14."

- Have the class announce the number of tens and the number of ones left over.

DISCUSSION

For the Beginning of the Month

Introduce the Counting Tape on the first day of school, or as soon as possible. Explain that a square will be attached to the tape for each day children come to school this year. If you can't begin on the first day of school, be sure to put up a square for each day they have already been in school. Ask children to call out the number for you to write on each square, beginning with *one* for Day 1.

Estimating Ask children how far around the room they think the Counting Tape will stretch by the 100th day of school. They will consider this question several times in the months ahead, so record their thoughts for reference.

For Later in the Month

Once or twice a week, in addition to the counting and recording activities, engage children in considering some other questions. Different questions relating to the Counting Tape help children develop a variety

The Counting Tape on the first day of school.

of number concepts and see many relationships. Below are some sample questions. The list of possibilities is varied in order to provide a broad range of questions that can be adapted for use later in the year.

Counting, Comparing To develop number sense and language for comparing:

- What number came just before today's number?
- What day of school came just after Day 9?
- What day of school came just before Day 13?
- What day of school came between Day 2 and Day 4?
- Which amount is greater (more), 3 squares or 7 squares? How do you know?
- (Cover up a number in the first group of ten with one of the blank Counting Tape squares.) Can you guess the mystery number?

Place Value On Day 10 begin to model the language for the number of tens and the number of ones left over (1 group of ten and 0 left over) to foster understanding of grouping by tens:

- How many groups of ten do we have so far?
- How many squares are left over?
- How do we record Day 16? (1 group of ten and 6 leftover ones)

Addition and Subtraction Concepts To encourage counting on and counting back:

- What day of school will it be in 1 more day?
- What day of school was it 2 school days ago?
- How many days have we come to school since the 10th day?

Patterns To encourage sorting and searching for patterns:

- What patterns do you see?
- What are the colors for the first ten days?
- How are the squares that come after 10 different from the first 10 squares? How are they alike?
- Is there anything that keeps happening over and over again?

Problem Solving, Communicating The purpose of asking these types of questions is to foster the children's thinking. By frequently following up responses with questions such as those below, you can encourage children to share their thinking.

- Would someone be willing to share how you got your answer?
- How did you figure this out?

In the beginning of kindergarten, only a few children may choose to try to explain how they solved a problem. As children experience more questions similar to these posed throughout the year, they will develop the confidence to share their strategies for problem solving. Occasionally you may want to describe your way as one way. Then ask if anyone has a different way.

HELPFUL HINTS

- Using lighter-colored squares for the tens and adding a yellow dot sticker to the center of the zero in numerals 10, 20, 30, and so on, helps to make the tens stand out. Some teachers draw on a face and name the zero, Zero the Hero. Children begin to anticipate its appearance every ten days.

- Some teachers find it difficult to continue the linear Counting Tape around the room. If this is a concern, consider creating a tape from 1–50 on your board and then adding numbers 51–100 below your board. By ending on the100th day, there are still many numbers for the children to see and talk about.

- If you have parent volunteers or older students to help with preparation, you might want to consider the special appeal of animal or object cutouts, for example, cutouts of a tugboat or kite. One teacher, Linda Anderson of New Orleans, had turtles lining up around her classroom one year. On the 100th day, the 100th turtle became a true standout when the children decorated its shell with 100 sequin "jewels."

Zero the Hero

Zero the Hero is so cool,

Zero the Hero comes to school!

Zero the Hero saves a space,

So all the other numbers

Will stay in their place!

Sing Zero the Hero to the tune of Three Little Fishies (Itty Bitty Pool).

Number & Operations	Algebra	Geometry	Measurement	Data & Probability
Problem Solving	Reasoning	Communication	Connections	Representation

CLIP COLLECTION

Concepts & Skills

- Develop number sense
- Sequence numbers
- Count with one-to-one correspondence
- Match quantities with numerals
- Count on and count back
- Count and group by tens and ones

Materials for the Year

12" × 18" piece of paper, 200 large paper clips, push pins, 0–9 Digit Cards (TR3)

Author Notes

"The Clip Collection provides children with a concrete model for counting sequentially, counting on and back, matching quantities with numerals, and grouping by tens. This element involves adding one paper clip to a chain each day of school. When the number of clips on a chain reaches ten, a new chain begins. On the 100th day of school, children will be able to count and see that a group of 100 paper clips is the same as 10 groups of ten clips. The Clip Collection is not intended to be a place value mat, but simply a way to organize a quantity into groups of ten. In later months, as the Clip Collection is used with the Counting Tape, children can match quantities with numerals. For September the visual model helps the children see that the number of clips increases as the number of days in school increases."

Ongoing Assessment

1. How many clips do we have in our Collection today?

2. How many clips do we have in our Collection if we take off 1 clip?

3. How many more clips do we need to make another group of ten?

Daily Routine

- Begin the Clip Collection on the first day of school if possible, by pinning a single paper clip to the far left side of a large piece of paper.

- Use Digit Cards made from TR3 to label the quantity with the numeral *1*.

- Each day of school for the rest of the month, add one clip to the previous day's clip, creating a chain of clips.

- Have the class count the clips together, then update the Digit Card numeral.

- On days 11, 21, 31, and so on, begin a new chain of clips to the right of the one just completed. Have the class tell how many groups of ten and how many leftover clips they see as you record the tens and ones digits.

Clip Collection on Day 16

DISCUSSION

For the First Day of School

On the first day of school, tell children that 1 clip will be added to the Collection each day they come to school this year. After pinning up the first clip, ask children what will happen tomorrow. Explain that tomorrow's Clip Collection will have 2 clips hanging from the pin.

For the Eleventh Day of School

Introduce children to counting by tens and ones during this discussion. Engage them in answering simple questions about the Clip Collection to promote number sense and thinking about number relationships.

Sample Dialogue

Teacher: Before I add today's clip to the chain, how many clips have we collected?

Class: We have 10.

Teacher: Let's count together and clap when we say *ten.*

Class: 1, 2, 3, 4, 5, 6, 7, 8, 9, 10 (clap).

Teacher: Yes, we have 10 clips on the chain. Did we need to count them?

Child: No. Yesterday we had 10 clips on the chain, and the chain is the same today.

Teacher: When I put up today's clip, beginning a new chain, how many clips will we have?

Child: We will have 11.

Teacher: Yes, 10 and 1 more is 11. (Add the clip.) Let's count them together. Remember to clap when we say *ten.*

Class: 1, 2, 3, 4, 5, 6, 7, 8, 9, 10 (clap), 11.

Teacher: Does our numeral match our Clip Collection?

Class: No.

Teacher: What do we need to do?

Child: We need to change the 0 to a 1.

MORE ▶

"Ten and 1 more is 11."

Teacher: (after the numeral has been changed) Now we have 11 clips and our numeral is 11; 1 group of ten and 1 leftover one. Let's talk about another way to count our Clip Collection. How many clips are in the first chain?

Child: There are 10.

Teacher: Yes. How many clips are in the new chain?

Child: We have 1.

Teacher: Let's try counting that together. This time we'll start by saying *ten* for the 10 clips in this chain.

Class: 10 (clap), 11.

For Later in the Month

Throughout the month, continue to discuss the Clip Collection. Count by ones and tens. In addition, use the Clip Collection to explore a variety of number relationships, develop skills in grouping, practice counting on and back, and solve problems. Frequent discussions promote an understanding of conservation of number—that a group of ten today will be a group of ten tomorrow. Since some children may be able to grasp this and others may not, there is a constant need to revisit this concept.

Also, careful questioning about the Clip Collection can provide an assessment in an informal setting. While numbers are still small, provide children with the opportunities to count a specific quantity by tens and then verify the amount by counting by ones. This will help children understand that there is more than one way to count and group a quantity. This list of sample questions is varied and can be adapted for use on any school day.

Place Value To develop number sense by counting and grouping:

• How many clips do we have in our Collection today? Do our numerals match our Clip Collection?

• How many chains of ten do we have? How many clips are left over?

Addition and Subtraction Concepts To develop mental math skills:

• How many clips will we have in our Collection tomorrow when we add 1 more clip?

• How many more clips do we need to make another group of ten?

• How many clips do we have in our Collection if we take off 1 clip? What if we take off all the "leftover" clips?

• How many clips do we have in our Collection if we take off 1 full chain of ten clips?

HELPFUL HINTS

• Plastic-coated paper clips are available in a variety of colors. Some teachers use five of one color and five of a second color for each chain to help children see six, seven, eight, nine, and ten at a glance.

• Flip cards can be made using rings to hold the Digit Cards into packets. Each day as the Clip Collection number changes, a Digit Card can be flipped over to record the new day's total.

GRAPH

Concepts & Skills

- Know the months of the year in order
- Understand ordinal position
- Count, compare, and order small quantities
- Collect and record data
- Create and interpret a picture graph

Materials for the Month

12 Birthday Baskets (TR4); Present Picture (TR4) for each child; tape, pins, or tacks; a list of birthdays of all the children in the class; marking pen; samples of two rectangular solids and a cylinder to model Present Picture shapes; 12 envelopes; small paper bag

Author Notes

"The Every Day Graph will offer a different opportunity each month for the class to gather, organize, and analyze data. In the first month, the class creates a Birthday Graph that will be displayed and referred to throughout the year. In future months, Birthday Data will be part of the Calendar element.

The Birthday Data display provides a rich resource of organized data of special interest to children. Sequenced from January to December, the Baskets help children learn the names and order of the months in a year. In other months, children will graph other information collected from surveys, class collections, weather observations, and probability experiments. Each graph offers children math they can see and talk about, providing frequent opportunities for counting, making comparisons, and doing mental math."

Setup

- Cut out and prepare 12 Birthday Baskets (TR4) by shading or outlining each in a different color. Label each with the name of a different month.
- Label each envelope with the name of one month.
- Cut out one Present Picture (TR4) for each child.

Daily Routine

- **On the first day** of school, place the Present Pictures in a bag and allow each child to select one to color. Label each present with the child's first name and birth date.
- Have the children bring you their Present Pictures when you call their birthday month. Place the pictures in the labeled envelopes.
- Help children place this month's Present Pictures on the Calendar in order. Post the month's empty Basket near the Calendar. When a birthday arrives, return the Present Picture to the Basket.

September Birthday Data

Carmen's birthday is September 15.

Ongoing Assessment

1. How many children have birthdays this month?

2. Which Basket has the most presents?

3. How many presents in this Basket are rectangular boxes?

- **On the second day**, take out January's Birthday Present Pictures and attach them to January's Birthday Basket. Post the Basket on the wall or board.

- Proceed chronologically, filling one new Basket each day. When the Graph is completed, all the Baskets should be displayed somewhere in the classroom in order from January to December, minus the current month.

- Discuss the increasing data each day for a minute or two.

- Occasionally invite children to make observations relating the shapes of the presents to the shapes of the three-dimensional solids.

- At the end of the month return the Basket to its place in the display.

DISCUSSION

For the Beginning of the Month

Problem Solving As children hunt for the correct spot on the Calendar for each present, they may need to count each day's space to figure out which space is the right one. To help them with this task, temporarily place a few Calendar Pieces on the Calendar as landmarks. Repeating this in the months to come will foster children's understanding of sequencing and their ability to order numbers.

For Throughout the Month

Number Sense The Birthday Baskets and Present Pictures offer experiences in counting, comparing, and ordering numbers. Some children will have already found their names and noticed whether their month's Basket has only a few or many pieces. The following sample questions encourage children to share their observations.

- How many children have birthdays this month?

- What do you think the number on each present means?

- How many presents are in your month's Birthday Basket?

- Which Basket has the most presents?

- Are there any months with no birthdays?

- Can you find two Baskets with the same number of presents?

- How many Baskets have just 1 present?

Revisiting variations of these sample questions helps children develop the confidence to share their observations and the strategies they used to figure out their responses.

Days of the Week, Months of the Year To practice the order of the months, have children occasionally join you in chanting the names of the months, beginning with January. Repeat the sequence, stopping with a clap on the current month. Point out the month's ordinal position in the year. Help children recognize that the first month of school is not the first month of the year.

Three-dimensional Shapes The Present Pictures for the Birthday Baskets provide an opportunity for introducing three-dimensional geometric objects — two different rectangular solids and a cylinder. As you hold up each of the three different Present Pictures, also have matching solids available for the children to see. Discussions similar to the following may help children identify the attributes of these objects.

September Birthday Data on the Calendar

Months of the Year Song

There are 12 months,
There are 12 months,
There are 12 months in a year;

January, February, March, April
May and June,
July, August, September, October,
No-vember, December.

There are 12 months,
There are 12 months,
There are 12 months in a year.

The months of the year can be sung to the tune of *Clementine*.

Sample Dialogue

Teacher: The Birthday Present Pictures for our graph come in different shapes. Let's look at the presents. (Hold up a shirt-box shape and the Present Picture representing it.) What do you see?

Child: A box.

Teacher: Yes, it is a box shape. Let's look at it again. What does it look like when it's turned over? What's different?

Child: It looks skinny now.

Teacher: What does it look like if I turn it again?

Child: Now it looks flat.

Teacher: That's right. When we turn this box in different directions we see different sides or different faces. Some faces of this box are skinny rectangles and some are wider rectangles. Let's look at this present. (Hold up a Present Picture and the other nearly cube-shaped rectangular solid it represents.) What do you see?

Child: Just a box. It's not flat or skinny.

Teacher: What does it look like when I turn it this way?

Child: Still not flat.

Teacher: As I turn the box, do you see different shaped faces or do all the faces have the same shape?

Child: They look the same.

Child: They are a little bit different.

Teacher: When I turn the box you can see different sides or faces, but none of them are skinny. So we have two different shaped boxes. (Hold up a Present Picture and a real cylinder that it represents.) Now let's look at this present. What do you see here?

Child: A can.

Child: A circle.

Teacher: And here's another circle on the other end. We have 2 circles. This shape that's like a can is called a cylinder.

"The Birthday Present Pictures come in different shapes."

Introduce three-dimensional objects that match the Present Pictures.

HELPFUL HINTS

- The Birthday Baskets might go anywhere — over the chalkboard, above a bulletin board, along a window, or on a wall. If possible allow enough space for the Baskets to be arranged in a single long row to emphasize the order of the months most clearly.

- Many children are disappointed if they are unable to celebrate their summer birthdays with the class. It is a good idea to choose an "unbirthday" for each of these children, perhaps six months before their real birthday on the same day of the month.

- Referring to a Basket by its color helps children identify the month. For example, "How many presents are in the green March Basket?"

Every Day Calendar

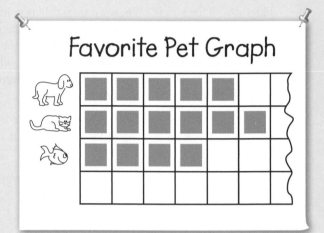

Graph

Daily Depositor

Birthday Baskets

| 17 | 18 | 19 | 20 | 21 | 22 | 23 | 24 | 25 | 26 | 27 | 28 | 29 | 30 | 31 | 32 |

Counting Tape

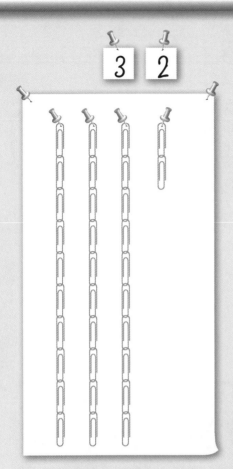

Clip Collection

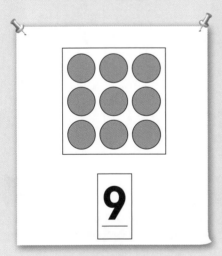

Domino Number Builder

This month the Domino Number Builder will be introduced, which allows the children to explore the quantities and numbers 1 to 9. Number stories accompany Domino Number Builder to provide exposure to using everyday language to tell number stories based on what children see in the dot configurations. Another new element, Daily Depositor, makes use of the days of the month. Children explore numbers 1 to 31 by seeing a variety of materials arranged in groups of tens and ones.

CALENDAR

Concepts & Skills

- Know the days of the week in order
- Know the names of the months
- Count on and count back
- Read, compare, and order numbers 1 to 31
- Understand and use position words
- Recognize, analyze, and extend patterns
- Solve problems and use mental math

Ongoing Assessment

1. How many Birthday Presents are in October's Basket?

2. Today is October ___, so what do you think tomorrow will be?

3. What do you think tomorrow's piece will look like?

Materials for October

Red and orange connecting cubes; assorted classroom art supplies such as construction paper, felt cutouts or old crayons

Author Notes

"To help children broaden their concept of pattern beyond the Calendar, have them occasionally interpret the month's AAAB pattern using body motions. Have children suggest one body movement to go with red and another to go with orange. Then the pattern "red, red, red, orange" might translate to "clap, clap, clap, stomp." By letting the body motion pattern continue on its own momentum even after the Calendar Pieces have run out, children can feel the strong predictability of pattern. Encourage children to suggest and try out two or three different interpretations of the pattern within a session.

In addition to translating patterns into body motions, at least once a week provide the children with opportunities to use classroom materials to copy and extend the month's pattern independently. Allow children to line up construction paper pieces, colored blocks, felt cutouts or old crayons to copy and extend the month's pattern.

Also provide red and orange connecting cubes for the children to copy the month's pattern. Throughout this month and in the months to come, use a variety of language to describe these cube patterns. For example, invite the children to describe the pattern using names of fruit, vegetables, or animals. This month's cube pattern might be represented as "apple, apple, apple, orange." This language also serves as an entry into later descriptions of patterns with letters."

The October Calendar Pieces create an AAAB pattern using red and orange leaves.

Daily Routine

- **The first day** post the October Month Strip on the Calendar.
- Place the first Calendar Piece on the calendar. If the first day of the month is a weekend day, post the Calendar Pieces through the current date with the children.
- Place October's Birthday Basket near the Calendar. Ask the children to predict where each present will appear on the Calendar, and then place them in the correct spots.

- **After the first day** add one Calendar Piece each day. Each Monday, add the weekend Pieces.
- Repeat the chants of the days of the week and the months of the year learned in September. (See Calendar, page 19, and, Birthday Graph, page 28.) Say the day's date all together.
- When a birthday arrives, return the present to the Basket.
- Once a week, ask discussion questions to help children describe what they see.
- Occasionally have children act out the pattern with body motions.

DISCUSSION

For the First Day

The following examples are the kinds of questions that draw out children's observations.

Counting, Comparing To foster counting and comparing:
- How many Birthday Presents are in October's Basket?
- How many Birthday Presents are can-shaped (cylinders)? Box-shaped?
- Which Basket has more Presents, September's or October's? How many more?
- Can you find any Baskets that have the same number of Presents as October's Basket?
- Can you find any Baskets that have more Presents than October's Basket? Fewer Presents?
- Are there any months with no birthdays?
- Where is this month's Basket in the arrangement of all the months?
- January is the first month and February is the second month. What month is October? (Let's count to figure this out.)

For After the Second Week

Explain that a pattern is beginning to appear on the October Calendar. Present discussion questions similar to those listed for the September Calendar (on pages 19–20). Other questions that encourage observations and sharing include the following.

Algebraic Thinking To search for patterns:
- Today is October ___, so what do you think tomorrow might be?
- What do you think tomorrow's piece will look like? (Some children may focus on the color of the next leaf, the shape of the next leaf, or the position of the stem on the next leaf.)
- Would someone tell us how you figured this out?
- Could someone share a different way that helped you?
- How are the pieces that we have put up the same? How are they different?
- Is a pattern happening over and over on this month's Calendar?
- Who would like to suggest two motions we can use to act out this pattern?

Present Pictures on the Calendar

"What color do you think tomorrow's piece will be?"

To Sum Up

At the end of the month, ask children to describe some of the things they have noticed about the Calendar this month. Some of their responses may include the following:

- The pattern was red, red, red, orange, red, red, red, orange.
- There are more red leaves than orange leaves.
- The pattern is stem down, stem down, stem down, stem up, and then it repeats.
- It goes fat leaf, fat leaf, fat leaf, skinny leaf over and over again.
- The oranges go down like stairs.
- It goes 3 reds and then 1 orange.

You might want simply to discuss the children's observations. You could also write children's observations in speech bubbles with their names and attach the bubbles to a large sheet of butcher paper, or poster board, which includes a smaller version of the Calendar (TR2).

HELPFUL HINTS

- At this time don't worry about children who are not getting the idea of patterns. Month after month of experiencing patterns and listening to the observations of their peers will help them. Ignore the stomp that should have been a clap. By asking everyone to make predictions, but asking only volunteers to share their reasoning, children who do not yet see patterns should not feel put on the spot.
- Children who copy the AAAB pattern easily with red and orange manipulatives may be ready to create a pattern choosing their own A and B colors or drawing pictures that repeat this sequence. Encourage children to be inventive while making sure they can duplicate the pattern.

Maria: "The oranges go down like stairs."
Louis: "The pattern was red, red, red, orange."
John: "It goes three reds and then orange."
Anna: "There were more reds than oranges."

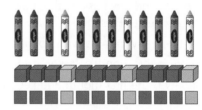

Patterns made with classroom materials

Number & Operations	Algebra	Geometry	Measurement	Data & Probability
Problem Solving	Reasoning	Communication	Connections	Representation

DAILY DEPOSITOR

Concepts & Skills

- Count with one-to-one correspondence
- Match quantities and numerals
- Read numerals to 31
- Group and count by tens and ones
- Sort by one attribute

Materials For the Year

The Depositor Poster and 0–9 Digit Cards (TR3). Also for this month: four 3" × 6" clear pockets and 31 buttons, small rocks, or counters.

Ongoing Assessment

1. How many counters do we have in this pocket?
2. How many groups of ten do we have today?
3. How many more days until we can make another group of ten?

Author Notes

"The Daily Depositor displays a number of counters equal to the day of the month, grouped by tens and ones. Starting on the first day of the month, a counter is added each day to the ones Depositor. When 10 counters have been collected they are moved over as one group of ten to the tens Depositor. Each month on the 10th, 20th, and 30th, children observe the digit in the tens place change to match the number of tens in the Depositor—helping children see numerals as a means of recording real-life quantities.

This month the Daily Depositor will collect a counter a day in a clear pocket on the ones side. Whenever ten are collected, they are removed and placed into an empty pocket, which is then pinned to the tens side. Each day the collection is counted and the total number of tens and ones are recorded above the Depositor. The collection can be used for sorting and counting games at month's end when it is removed from the Depositor."

Daily Depositor on October 12

Daily Routine

• Each day of the month add 1 counter to the ones Depositor. On Mondays, add counters for Saturday, Sunday, and Monday so the total is always the same as the day of the month.

• Count the total and record the number in the ones place above the Depositor.

• **On the 10th**, when 10 counters have been collected, remove them all and place them in a new pocket. Then pin this pocket to the tens side. Discuss this special place for the groups of ten.

• Have the class tell how many groups of ten they see, and how many loose ones.

• Record the amount above the Depositor as 1 group of ten and 0 leftover ones.

• **On the 11th**, put a counter in the ones pocket and continue the pattern of updating established in the first 10 days.

• On the 20th and 30th, move a new group of ten to the tens side again.

DISCUSSION

For Throughout the Month
Sample Dialogue

Teacher: How many counters do we have in the Depositor today?

Class: We have 25.

Teacher: How can you be sure there are 25?

Child: We can count them. 1, 2, 3, . . . , 25.

Teacher: Could we start by counting the groups of tens?

Teacher & Class: 10, 20 (clap), 21, 22, 23, 24, 25.

Teacher: Did anyone count them a different way?

Child: I started on 10 and counted them all on my fingers.

Teacher: Okay, let's try that. Here's 10. Now let's count the ones in the other group of ten.   **MORE ▶**

Teacher	
& Class:	11, 12, 13, 14, 15, 16, 17, 18, 19, 20.
Teacher:	Now the extra ones in the ones pocket.
Class:	21, 22, 23, 24, 25.
Teacher:	I'll write 2 for the two groups of ten that made 20 on the tens side and 5 on the ones side. Let's read it together.
Teacher	
& Class:	Two groups of ten and 5 ones is 25.
Teacher:	How many more days until we can make another group of ten?

"Two groups of ten and 5 is 25."

To Sum Up

At the end of the month, the 31 counters can be removed from the Depositor and used for sorting and counting games. To introduce these activities, gather children in a circle so they can see them well.

Sorting If you used rocks spread the collection out so the children can see them and ask questions to help children notice different ways to sort. Have a couple volunteers sort the rocks into two piles. Then push the rocks back together and ask for another sorting suggestion.

- Would someone like to tell us one thing you notice about the rocks when you look at them?

- Yes, some are shiny. Are they all shiny? Would you like to help sort these rocks into shiny and not-shiny piles?

- Can anyone tell us something else you notice about the rocks?

- Continue sorting the same materials over and over again as long as interest and time allow. Children will discover how the objects are alike and different and increase their descriptive vocabulary by listening to each other's observations.

Counting, Comparing When the objects have been sorted, occasionally ask, to encourage comparing:

- Which group has more? How many more?

- When the amounts are close in number, have volunteers line up the groups in one-to-one correspondence or count to compare the quantities. This is a good opportunity to talk about arranging objects so that they are easier to count, a lead-in to graphing.

"Some are **big**."

"Some are **not big**."

HELPFUL HINTS

- *Can You Guess How We Sorted?* Children who choose to sort the counters often enjoy having others try to guess how they have sorted the collection. After some children have sorted, gather a few problem-solvers around the results. Ask them to look at the two piles to see if they can find some way that all the objects in one of the piles are alike. Perhaps one of the groups has all the dark rocks, or all the big ones, or all the smooth ones. Are these missing from the other pile? It's fun to search for the characteristic that separates the two groups.

- Sorting activities are fun for parents and children to try at home. Home collections and small toys work well.

- See page 77 for the January *Collect and Count* activity. The first player to collect 15 is the winner.

"Can You Guess How We Sorted?"

DOMINO NUMBER BUILDER

Concepts & Skills

- Count with one-to-one correspondence
- Recognize small quantities
- Compare and order quantities to 9
- Visualize domino arrangements for 1 through 9
- Match quantities and numerals
- See sets from 1 to 9 as combinations of smaller sets

Materials for October

9 Domino Records (TR7), 2 markers, (1 black permanent marker and 1 blue watercolor marker or crayon), 0–9 Digit Cards (TR3), 9 paper clips

Author Notes

"Domino Number Builder activities present children with the opportunity to develop instant recognition of small sets up to 9. A new quantity in a new arrangement of dots is created on each of nine days. This presents the class with a changing visual display of the quantities 1 to 9. In later months, combinations for these numbers are also explored. The main purpose of this activity is to help children become familiar with sets to 9 and to see relationships among these numbers. This happens as the teacher and children offer stories that go with each day's new arrangement of dots. When the discussions are open-ended and divergent thinking is encouraged, the Dominoes may sometimes spark stories that involve adding, subtracting, or comparing numbers. For example, on the fifth day of creating Dominoes, stories might include "I have 3 pennies and Michael has 2. We have 5 altogether." It is important to be open to any stories that describe relationships that children see. Children who make these kinds of observations in kindergarten are developing number sense critical to their success with primary mathematics."

Daily Routine

- Each day on nine different days outline circles on a Domino Record (TR7) with a black marker to create the arrangement for the day. For example, on the fourth day, outline dots in the four corners of the Domino Record.
- Have a volunteer color the dots blue and post the Domino Record on the bulletin board. Display only one Domino Record at a time.
- Attach the appropriate Digit Card below the Domino Record with a paper clip.
- Have volunteers discuss what they see. Periodically have the children tell stories and record their stories on blank paper to post on the bulletin board.
- Engage children in a variety of activities to help develop instant recognition of small quantities and help children match quantities with numerals.

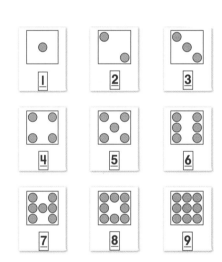

Dot arrangements for Dominoes 1–9

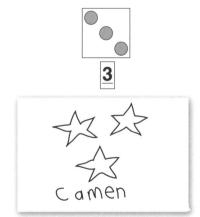

"I have 3 stars on my shoe."

Ongoing Assessment

1. Quick as you can, how many dots are on this Domino?
2. Can you tell me a story about this Domino?
3. The next Domino will have one more dot. How many dots will that be?

DISCUSSION

For the Beginning of the Month

A conversation similar to the following might occur on the third day that a Domino Record is filled in.

Sample Dialogue

Teacher: How many dots did we color in on this Domino, yesterday?

Child: We colored two.

Teacher: Today we are going to color a new Domino with one more dot than yesterday. How many dots do you think we are going to color?

Child: Three dots.

Teacher: I will outline 3 dots. Would someone like to volunteer to color the 3 dots with my blue marker so we can all see them? While that is being done, who would like to share a story about 3?

Child: My little brother is 3 years old.

Teacher: Great! Anyone else?

Child: I have 3 loose teeth.

Child: We have 3 kids in our family.

Teacher: These are good stories. Now let's hang the numeral 3 card from our Domino and trace this 3 in the air.

For Later in the Month

When all nine Dominoes have been colored, the activities described in Helpful Hints will extend the use of the Dominoes throughout the month.

HELPFUL HINTS

- Play *Mix and Match.* Spread out all of the Dominoes and all the Digit Cards. Have two volunteers match the dominoes with the appropriate Digit Card. Then scramble them up again and play again.

- Play *Quick as You Can.* Encourage instant recognition by using the Domino Records as flash cards on a ring. Hold one up and ask children to say its name as quickly as they can. Invite volunteers to convince the children of the quantity shown (I know it is 4 because 2 and 2 make 4). Then ask a child to be the "teacher" and flash the Domino Records.

- Some teachers like to make a set of giant Dominoes (TR26) labeled with the numeral and the number word to display permanently.

- Asking children to share what they see lets them reflect on the configuration, rather than the amount. For example, a child may describe the configuration of four dots as a box. This helps other children visually recall that domino.

- You may want to have real dominoes in your classroom so that children can see where these configurations originate. Be sure to allow children the opportunity to explore the dominoes before using them for any other purpose.

Mix and Match Game

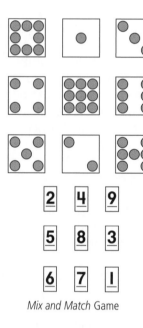

Giant Domino, numeral, and number word display

COUNTING TAPE AND CLIP COLLECTION

Concepts & Skills

- Sequence numbers
- Count with one-to-one correspondence
- Count and group by tens and ones
- Match quantities with numerals
- Compare and order quantities
- Count on and count back
- Discover number patterns and use mental math

Daily Routine

- Beginning this month update and discuss the Counting Tape and Clip Collection at the same time.
- Each day, attach one numbered square to the Counting Tape (continue the same color sequence) and add one clip to the Clip Collection. Update the Digit Cards to reflect the total number of clips.
- Review the number of days in school using the Clip Collection and point out that number on the Counting Tape.
- Discuss more frequently early in the month to take advantage of the smaller numbers.

DISCUSSION

For the Beginning of the Month

Addition and Subtraction Concepts While the Clip Collection is still small, short, frequent discussions help children develop number sense. These sample questions will help children develop the concepts of one more, one less, ten more, and ten less.

- How many clips do we have in our Collection today?
- How many chains of ten do we have? How many clips are left over?
- How many clips do we have in our Collection if I take off 1 clip? If I take off 5 clips?
- How many clips do we have in our collection if I take down 1 full chain of ten clips?

You may adapt these questions as well as the September Counting Tape questions to use later in the month with greater Counting Tape numbers and greater Clip Collection quantities.

> **Ongoing Assessment**
> 1. How many clips do we have in our Collection today?
> 2. How many clips do we have in our Collection if I take down one full chain of ten clips?
> 3. What day of school will it be in 2 days?

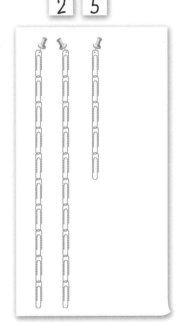

Clip Collection on Day 25

For Later In the Month

Using the Counting Tape and Clip Collection, children develop number sense, language for comparing, understanding of grouping, counting on, counting back, and sorting and pattern search strategies. Have children count by tens and ones using the Clip Collection and repeat using the Counting Tape. The questions you ask may prompt children to find answers using the Counting Tape and/or the Clip Collection. Have children share the way they found their answers using either or both elements.

Counting, Comparing Here are some sample questions you may use to develop number sense and the language of comparing:

- Which came first, Day 13 or Day 15?
- What number came just before today's number? (So, 24 is one less than 25.)
- What number will come just after today's number? (So, 26 is one more than 25.)
- What day of school came just before Day 5? Just before Day 15? Just before Day 25?
- What day of school came between Day 11 and Day 13? Between Day 21 and Day 23?
- How many more than 20 is 25?

Place Value To promote understanding of grouping:

- How many groups of ten do we have so far? How many extra ones?
- How many clips are left if we take off the first chain of ten?
- How many squares would we have on the Counting Tape if we took off the first group of ten?

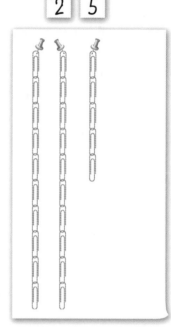

"How many more than 20 is 25?"

Addition and Subtraction Concepts To encourage counting on and counting back:

- What day of school will it be in 2 days?
- What day of school was it 2 days ago?
- How many more days until the 28th day of school?
- How many days have we come to school since the 20th day? Since the 15th day?

Patterns To encourage sorting and the search for patterns:

- How many more days until the color of the square will be the same as today's color?
- How are the squares in the 20s like the squares up to 10? How are they different?

HELPFUL HINTS

- To help children relate the numbers on the Counting Tape and in the Clip Collection to the numbers they use in their daily lives, play the game *Numbers, Numbers, Everywhere*. After Day 20, find some sets less than 20 which children can easily see or use. Give children a clue or brief description of the item(s) and have them guess what it is. For example, you might be thinking of four windows. One clue for the class might be, "Plants get good light when they are near these." Make sure children guess the objects and determine their number.

- Some teachers like to have children make their own representation of the Clip Collection every ten days. Using TR5, children can color a chain of ten clips. One teacher has children color the chains using the color pattern in the Counting Tape. Continue to label, collect, and save these for Day 100.

- Pairs of children can play the game *Collect Ten*. Make a copy of the Paper Clip Chain (TR5) to use as a game board. Cut it apart. Each child will need one ten-clip chain and ten counters. They will also need one penny. Players choose a counter color and then take turns flipping the penny and adding counters to their chain. For heads a player adds two counters and for tails one counter. Before each flip, the player must tell how many counters they already have and how many more they need to make ten. The game is over when a ten-clip chain is filled with ten counters. Empty the chain and play again.

"I have 8 counters. I need 2 more."

Number & Operations	Algebra	Geometry	Measurement	Data & Probability
Problem Solving	Reasoning	Communication	Connections	Representation

GRAPH

Concepts & Skills

- Collect and record data on a graph over time
- Read and interpret data on a picture or bar graph
- Count and compare small quantities

Materials for October

Every Day Graph (TR8), several $1\frac{3}{4}$" square paper markers in a bright color

Author Notes

"The Every Day Graph will be used to display the results of preference polls or class surveys. These provide a fun way for class members to become better acquainted and to learn about the opinions and preferences of their classmates. Begin a list of questions that the children have for one another. Add to this list throughout the year. Questions like the following encourage discussion:

- Which of these pets would you most like to have?
- Which of these three colors do you like best?
- Which of these two stories did you enjoy the most?
- Where would you rather play, inside or outside?
- How do you come to school?
- Which of these sports do you like the best?
- Do you have a baby in your family?
- Which of these ice cream flavors is your favorite?
- Do you have any sisters or brothers?

Ongoing Assessment

1. How many markers are on our graph in the longest row?
2. How many markers are on our graph in all?
3. Do we have enough markers now to know how the graph will turn out?

Later in the year, children may enjoy doing surveys of their own. Allow children to decide on their own survey questions and carry clipboards around, polling their classmates. Limiting the class to two pollsters for any one day keeps interruptions to the other children's pursuits to a minimum. Most children enjoy being asked to give their opinion or preference and having someone care enough to mark it down. The different polls form a display of considerable interest to the group, providing so many comparisons and so much to talk about."

Setup

- Use multiple copies of TR8 to set up a grid large enough to graph responses from everyone.

Daily Routine

- At the start of each week, gather data on a preference question. At first, offer just two choices as responses. In later weeks, offer three choices.

- Have each child prepare a colored square of paper that shows his or her preference. They might draw a picture, add a sticker, or write a word to indicate their choice. Collect the squares in a small paper bag. Add a square for yourself as well.

- Each day have a volunteer select 5 or 6 square markers and attach them to the Graph.

- Ask discussion questions related to the new data as the appearance of the Graph changes.

Favorite Pet Graph midweek

DISCUSSION

For the Start of Each Week

Collecting Data Present the children with the survey question chosen by you or the class. Ask for a show of hands indicating their choice. Point out that it is difficult to represent their choices in this manner (a show of hands) and that you have a way to organize this information that will help them to better see the results. Have children copy their choice from the possible answers onto their own squares. Tell them that they do not need to put their names on the squares. Explain to the children that some of the squares will be attached to the Graph each day until all the squares have been put up.

For the Rest of the Week

Analyzing Data After a volunteer has placed the first set of 5 or 6 square markers on the Graph, ask children if they can predict which choice will have the most squares when they are all up. Let children share their thinking. Each time another set of squares has been added, ask children if the new data change their thinking about what the entire graph will look like when everyone's square is up. Children may see that generalizing about the entire sample from too little data can lead them to jump to the wrong predictions.

Asking questions such as the following will encourage children to notice and describe the graph as it changes from day to day.

- Does the choice that had the most squares yesterday still have the most?
- Does another choice have more today?
- Is it likely that this choice will remain in the lead tomorrow? Are you certain?

For When the Graph Is Complete

Data When the graph is finally complete, focus the class on interpreting the data. Ask questions such as:

- What does our Graph tell us?
- What do we know about our choices from the Graph?

Fill in, if necessary, with some questions that help them see which choice was made by the greatest number and the least number of children. This is a good time to remind them that having different opinions makes the class interesting. Some other questions could include:

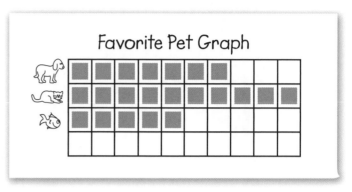

Favorite Pet Graph completed

- How many squares or markers are on our graph in the longest row?
- How many markers are in the shortest row?
- How many more markers are in the longest row than in the shortest row?
- How many markers are on our graph in all? Can anyone share how you got the total?
- Were ten markers enough for us to make a good guess?

HELPFUL HINTS

- When asking questions about a graph, it is helpful to allow for children who need some time to reflect without being influenced by quick responders. During these few seconds of thinking time, no one is allowed to call out an answer. After this quiet time some teachers elicit a group response. This is an easy way to become aware of the level of confidence in the class and the proportion of correct and incorrect answers without putting individuals on the spot.

- After children respond, turn the focus from the answers to the strategies different class members used to get their answers.

- It might be helpful to have wrap-up discussions on Fridays. You may want to write children's observations in speech bubbles with their names and post them around the graph.

- Some teachers may choose to write numbers along the bottom of the graph to make it easy to tell at a glance how many markers are in each row. This is a standard graphing practice in the upper grades. However, leaving these numbers off the graphs in kindergarten has the advantage that children get practice counting with one-to-one correspondence each time they want to find out how many.

Every Day Calendar

Birthday Baskets

2 5 stamps

November Temperature Graph

warm										
chilly, cool										
very cold										

Graph

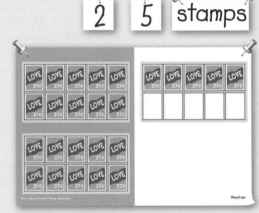

Daily Depositor

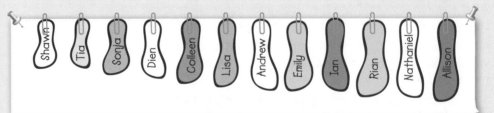

Estimation and Measurement

39 40 41 42 43 44 45 46 47 48 49 50 51 52 53 54 55 56

    Counting Tape

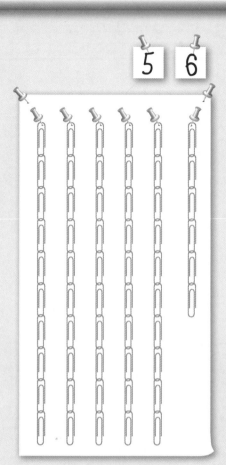

Clip Collection

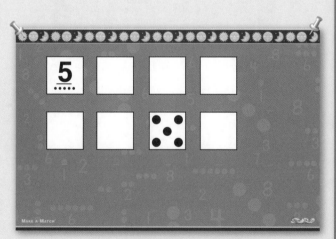

Domino Number Builder

NOVEMBER ELEMENTS

In November, one new element, Estimation and Measurement, is added to Calendar Math. This month children practice comparing lengths using children's feet. On the Calendar children are exposed to a variety of rectangles. A new Every Day Graph records children's choice of clothing for the day's temperature, and Domino Number Builder takes the form of a memory game. The Daily Depositor and the Clip Collection and Counting Tape both challenge children with even greater numbers.

CALENDAR

Concepts & Skills

- Know the days of the week and names of the months
- Count with one-to-one correspondence
- Count on and count back
- Read, compare, and order numbers 1 to 30
- Recognize, analyze, and extend patterns
- Solve problems and use mental math
- Explore and describe the attributes of rectangles

Ongoing Assessment

1. What day is today?
2. What is alike about all the red shapes?
3. What will the Calendar Piece that we put up in 3 days look like?

New Materials for the Rest of the Year

Yesterday Arrow Marker

Author Notes

"This month's pattern will allow many interpretations depending on the background of your children. The rectangles will be represented by an upright rectangle, the same rectangle rotated 90° (or a horizontal rectangle) and a square rectangle. (A square is a special rectangle.) By providing a variety of rectangles, children will have opportunities to move beyond the common representation of a four-sided figure with two horizontal long sides and to make generalizations about rectangles. Some children will simply refer to this pattern as a purple, red, purple, red pattern, others may see it as a circle, rectangle, circle, rectangle pattern, and still others may notice the different rectangles and use them in the description of the pattern. As long as the children describe the pattern unit as repeating, accept the various interpretations."

Daily Routine

- Continue the established routines.
- On the first school day of the month introduce the Yesterday Marker.
- Throughout the month have a volunteer name the day before today and place the Yesterday Marker above that day.
- Occasionally ask questions that lead children to see the similarities and differences between the shapes on the Calendar Pieces.

DISCUSSION

For the First Day

Introduce the Yesterday Marker. Explain that the day before today is called yesterday. Ask children to name today's day and place the Today Arrow Marker above the day. Then have a volunteer name the day before today and place the Yesterday Arrow Marker above that day.

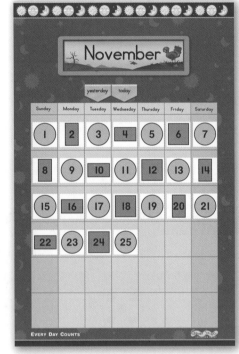

The November Calendar Pieces create an ABAB pattern with purple circles and three different red rectangles.

Problem Solving Place the November Birthday Basket near the Calendar. Ask the November birthday children to hold up their Present Pictures and ask volunteers to help arrange the birth dates in order. Let children predict where each birthday piece should be placed on the Calendar and ask volunteers to share how they made their predictions. Have children compare the number of box-shaped presents and cylinder-shaped presents this month.

For the Third Week

Algebraic Thinking Discuss the new pattern that is appearing on the November Calendar. Encourage children to interpret the month's ABAB pattern using motions. For example, someone might suggest putting hands above their head for the purple circles and putting hands at their waist for the red rectangles. Have the children create a pattern "train" with connecting cubes that translate the ABAB pattern on the Calendar.

To Sum Up

At the end of the month, ask children to describe some of the things they have noticed about the Calendar this month. Be sure to draw out some of the following ideas.

Two-dimensional Shapes To explore the attributes of circles, rectangles, and squares (square rectangles):

- What do you notice about all the purple shapes?
- Do you see other things in the room that have the same shape?
- How are all of the rectangles alike? How are they different?
- What do you notice about the sides of the square?
- How many squares do you see on the Calendar?

Algebraic Thinking To search for patterns:

- Tell us about anything that you notice in this month's pattern.
- Why is this a pattern?
- (Turn over a Calendar Piece and invite children to convince others of the shape and color of the hidden piece.) What shape or color do you think the hidden Calendar Piece is?

You may want to discuss the children's observations of the Calendar and its pattern or record the observations as described in October (page 34).

HELPFUL HINTS

- Sometimes, when you are chanting the color pattern on the Calendar or doing body motions, change to saying "ABABABAB" or other verbal descriptions while following the pattern. This helps some children see the pattern.
- Using the term *square rectangle* for all squares can help the children understand that all squares really are special rectangles. You might instead choose to use *square rectangle* only occasionally or not at all, based on what your children seem ready for.

Karen: *"Red always follows purple."*

Nunti: *"It's an ABABAB pattern."*

Jon: *"I see slanted stripes."*

Birthday Present Picture in place

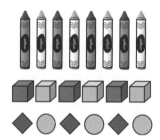

Pattern "trains"

DAILY DEPOSITOR

Concepts & Skills

- Count with one-to-one correspondence
- Match quantities and numerals
- Read and write numerals to 30
- Group and count by fives and tens
- See combinations for 5 and 10

Special Materials for November

A collection of 31 canceled stamps; 2 Double Ten Grids (TR6); glue stick or pins

Author Notes

"This month the Daily Depositor continues to use the place-value mat format. Stamps will be collected one per day on an empty Ten Grid attached to the ones side of the Depositor. Establish, by counting with the class, that this grid has 5 spaces on the top row and 5 spaces on the bottom row. The Ten Grid arrangement makes it easy to see the number of stamps at a glance. Each day children focus on combinations for 5 and 10 as they think about how many spaces remain to complete a row of five or the entire grid. On the tenth day of the month when the Ten Grid becomes full, it will be moved to the tens side of the Depositor and the number of tens and ones will be recorded above the respective mats."

Setup

- Attach a blank Ten Grid to the ones side of the Depositor.

Daily Routine

- **On the first day** of school in November have a volunteer paste one stamp in the first space of the top row of the Ten Grid, then record a 1 above the ones place on the Depositor.

- Continue adding a stamp each day. On Mondays, add a stamp for Saturday, Sunday, and Monday so the total is always the same as the day's date.

- Complete the top row on the fifth day of the month. On the sixth through the tenth, fill in the bottom row.

- Ask frequently, "How many stamps are still needed to fill in the entire Ten Grid?"

- **On November 10th,** move the full Ten Grid to the tens side. From here on, have children tell how many groups of ten and how many extra ones they see as you record the tens and ones digits above the Depositor.

- On the 11th, place a stamp on a new empty Ten Grid on the ones side and continue the pattern of updating daily.

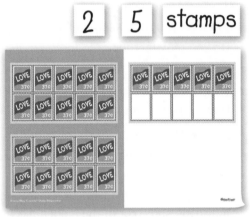

"How many more stamps do we need to fill the whole Ten Grid?"

Discussion

For the Middle of the Month

After adding the day's stamp to the Ten Grid, ask the children to discuss what they see. When the first Ten Grid is moved to the tens side, revisit the concept of a special place for the group of tens and a special place to collect the extra ones.

Sample Dialogue

Teacher: How many stamps do we see in all today?

Class: There are 24 stamps.

Teacher: Yes, 24. How do you know we have 24?

Child: I counted them.

Teacher: Let's all do that.

Teacher & Class: 1, 2, 3, 4, . . . , 24.

Teacher: Did anyone get 24 a different way?

Child: I counted the tens.

Teacher: Let's count by tens.

Class: 10, 20, (clap) 21, 22, 23, 24.

Teacher: Let me record that. I'll write a *2* for the 2 groups of tens and a *4* for the extra ones. How many more stamps do we need to fill the top row of five?

Class: We need 1 more.

Teacher: Yes, 4 and 1 more are 5. How many stamps do we need to fill the whole Ten Grid?

Child: We need 6—1 for the top row and 5 more is 6.

Teacher: Yes. We need 6 more stamps to make 10. On what day of the month will this Ten Grid become full? Will it be a school day or a weekend day?

Helpful Hints

- At the end of November, cut up the Ten Grids so children can use the stamps for sorting and counting games. To introduce sorting with the stamps, see page 36. Children will notice many attributes to sort by when they examine the stamps—those with animals, faces, buildings, flowers or plants, flags, words, some that are red, and so on. Children enjoy having you and others try to guess the characteristic by which they have sorted.

- To use a *Collect and Count* activity, see January, page 77. Instead of bundling tens, let children place the stamps they collect on blank Ten Grids.

- Children might like to make their own stamp collector's books by pasting an empty Ten Grid on each of several blank sheets of paper and stapling the pages together. Collecting and organizing stamps might make a fun winter break project.

DOMINO NUMBER BUILDER

Concepts & Skills

- Count with one-to-one correspondence
- Compare and order quantities to 9
- Visualize domino arrangements for 1 through 9
- Match quantities and numerals
- See sets from 1 to 9 as combinations of smaller sets
- Use spatial problem solving to match arrangements of dots with numerals
- Understand and use position words

Materials for November

1–9 Domino Halves (TR10), 1–9 Numeral Dot Cards (TR11),
Make a Match poster

Author Notes

"This month, the Domino Number Builder becomes a Make a Match memory game, giving the children a chance to match quantities and numerals using Domino Halves and Numeral Cards. Children engage in spatial problem solving, relying on visual memory to remember where each Domino and Numeral Card is in the arrangement of cards. Make a Match also helps children learn ordinal descriptions and other position language such as top row, bottom row, and in the middle, as you model the use of these words and they describe the location of the two cards they wish to turn over. Dominoes and numerals 1 through 4 are explored until all matches are made and then dominoes and numerals 5 through 9 are placed on the poster for matching. Each day, the children continue to turn over two cards until a match is found. This match is then removed from the board."

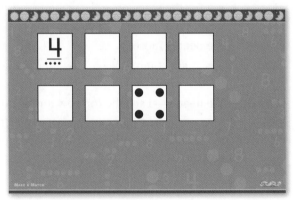

"They match!"

Setup

- Show the children the Domino Halves and the Numeral Dot Cards for 1 through 4 or 5 through 9 that they will be matching.
- Then randomly clip the cards onto the poster face down.

Daily Routine

- Each day play Make a Match until one match is made. When a match is made, remove the cards from the poster.
- To play, have a volunteer choose two cards to turn over. If they match, both cards are removed. If they do not match, they are replaced, face down. The next volunteer tries to make a match by turning over any two cards. The game continues for that day until one match is found.

DISCUSSION

For the Beginning of the Month

A conversation similar to the following might occur.

Sample Dialogue

Teacher: Today we are going to play a memory game with our Dominoes and the Numeral Dot Cards. Let's look at our cards. You will notice that some of our cards are dominoes and some are numerals. I am going to place these cards on the board and then you will get to search for the domino and the number card that matches. Who would like to be our first volunteer?

Child: I want to turn over this one.

Teacher: She is turning over the first card in the top row.

Child: It's a domino with 2 dots.

Teacher: Which card are you turning over next?

Child: I think that this one might match.

Teacher: She chose the last card in the bottom row. Is it a match?

Child: No, it's a number 3.

Teacher: What were you hoping to turn over?

Child: I wanted the number 2.

Teacher: Class, I will point to the cards. Will you tell us what you see? Do the dots match the number?

Class: No.

Teacher: Remember where these cards are placed. Let's turn them back over and try again for a match. Who wants to try?

Continue until a match is made. Remove the match from the board and continue the next day. When all matches have been made, discuss Dominoes and Numeral Dot Cards for numbers 5 through 9 and play Make a Match for those quantities.

For After Make a Match is Completed

Problem Solving, As in October, the Domino Records can be used for some fun *Guess My Domino* games to practice matching numerals with quantities. With all of the Domino Records displayed, give the children clues to identify a Domino Record. For example:

- I have more than three dots,
- I have fewer than seven dots, and
- I look like a square except I have a dot in the center.
  Which domino am I?

As the children develop vocabulary, let them ask questions to guess the domino. For example, they might ask:

- Is it a neighbor of 3?
- Does it look like 4 and 1 more?
- Is it more than 6?
- Is it 1 more than 3?

Other activities you might enjoy trying with your class that encourage children to use the language of math are included in Helpful Hints.

HELPFUL HINTS

- *Stack Match* Using connecting cubes or beans, ask each child to make stacks with the quantities 1 to 9. One volunteer holds up a Domino Card while children point to their stack of that quantity. The opposite game works as well. Hold up a card and ask students to make a stack equal to the quantity represented on that card.

- *Domino Comparing* Using 2 or 3 sets of Domino Cards, both children draw a card from the stack and turn it over. The child with the greater amount states the comparison, for example, "3 is more (greater) than 2" and takes both cards. Then both draw another card. This game can be modified so the player with the smaller number gets both cards after stating the comparison.

- *Make a Match* The children can also play their own version of Make a Match independently.

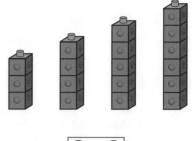

Stack Match: "Which stack matches this domino?"

| Number & Operations | Algebra | Geometry | Measurement | Data & Probability |
| Problem Solving | Reasoning | Communication | Connections | Representation |

COUNTING TAPE AND CLIP COLLECTION

Concepts & Skills

- Develop number sense
- Sequence numbers
- Count with one-to-one correspondence
- Count and group by tens and ones
- Match quantities with numerals
- Compare and order quantities
- Count on and count back
- Discover number patterns and use mental math
- Solve problems

Ongoing Assessment

1. What number did we put up 1 day after Day 34? What color is it?

2. What day came 1 day before Day 36?

3. Can you tell what day will come 1 day before Day 56?

New Materials for the Rest of the Year

Pairs of paper hands (TR12)

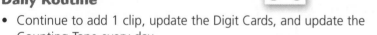

"What number did we put up 1 day after Day 34?"

Daily Routine

- Continue to add 1 clip, update the Digit Cards, and update the Counting Tape every day.

- Each time you reach a new multiple of ten, hang a pair of hands showing ten fingers under that number on the Tape, as the class counts the days of school by tens. The first time you do this, also go back and hang pairs of hands under previous multiples of ten.

© Great Source. Copying is prohibited.

- Discuss two or three times a week. Remove chains of ten as you ask the children to tell how many will be left. Count by ones to verify answers. Replace the chains before ending the discussion.

DISCUSSION

For Throughout the Month

Continue to involve children in comparing, counting on, counting back, and counting by tens and ones by adapting the sample questions of September and October to the greater numbers and larger quantities that appear this month. (See pages 23, 26, 39–40.)

Addition and Subtraction Concepts Use the Clip Collection to show 10 more than and 10 less than the day's number. Remove a chain of 10 clips from the Clip Collection and 41 becomes 31. Remove another full chain and ask children to predict what 31 becomes. Count by ones to verify. Repeat one more time and then reverse the process. Continue until you return to the current day's number.

Algebraic Thinking By the end of November, children will see the counting sequence from 1 to 10 repeated four or five times. Invite children to consider why a pair of hands is hung below each multiple of ten. Encourage them to use what they know about groups of ten and to look for patterns to answer these questions about the relationship of one number to another.

- Can you find Day 4 on the Tape?
- What number did we put up 1 day after Day 4? What color is it?
- What number did we put up 1 day after Day 14? What color is that?
- What number did we put up 1 day after Day 24? Day 34?
- Do you see anything alike about all our answers?
- Can you predict what day will come 1 day after Day 44?

On another day:
- What day came 1 day before Day 6? What is the color of that square?
- What day came 1 day before Day 16? Day 26? Day 36?
- Do you see anything alike about all our answers?
- Can you predict what day will come 1 day before Day 56?

HELPFUL HINT

- If the children have enjoyed the *Numbers, Numbers Everywhere* game mentioned in October Helpful Hints, play with higher numbers, such as 36 markers or 41 clips. Work with objects in quantities no greater than 50.

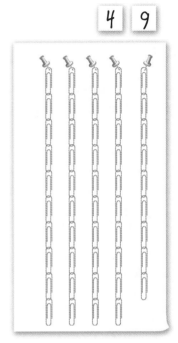

"How many clips do you think we will have tomorrow?"

GRAPH

Concepts & Skills

- Collect and record data on a graph over time
- Read and interpret data on a picture or bar graph
- Count and compare small quantities
- Understand temperature

Special Materials for November

Every Day Graph (TR8), Clothing Markers (TR13)

Author Notes

"The Graph offers a different opportunity each day for the class to gather, organize, and analyze data. In November, children will observe temperatures by determining which kind of clothing is appropriate to wear outdoors each day. Pictures of different clothing (TR13) associated with temperatures that feel hot, warm, chilly, cold, and very cold are available to make the Graph. In order to make the graph easier for the children to read and analyze, select three clothing markers that are appropriate for your year-round regional temperatures. With your class, decide on the color to use for the three piece of clothing to represent each. The class will record their decisions on picture graphs again in January and April, so be sure to keep the graph after the month ends."

Daily Routine

- Each day have the class talk about the temperature outside and how it is reflected in what they would wear outside.
- Have a volunteer attach the appropriate Clothing Marker to the Graph.
- Discuss the accumulating data few times each week.

DISCUSSION

For the First Day

It is best to make weather observations at a similar time each day, since morning and afternoon temperatures can vary a great deal. Instead of preparing the temperature Graph ahead of time, have children help you set it up. Tell children you have markers showing the different kinds of clothing people wear in different temperatures. Have them describe when they might wear some of the clothing pictured. A dialogue similar to the one that follows may help children think about temperature, consider how they feel in certain temperatures, and decide what types of clothing they would wear in hot, warm, chilly, cold or very cold weather.

November Temperature Graph

© Great Source. Copying is prohibited.

Sample Dialogue

Teacher: (Hold up a short-sleeved marker.) Can anyone tell me when we might wear a top like this one?

Child: I would wear it when it's warm, not hot.

Teacher: That's right, we wear short sleeves when it is warm. (Attach a short-sleeved marker to a strip of paper and write warm on it.) This strip says *warm*. (Hold up a sweater marker.) When might we wear a sweater?

Child: I'd wear it when I'm chilly.

Child: I might wear it when it's cool.

Teacher: Yes, many of us will put on sweaters when we feel chilly or cool. I will write *chilly* and *cool* on this strip of paper and attach a sweater marker to it. (Hold up a hat-and-mittens marker.) If we need to put on these, can you tell me what it is like outside?

Child: It's very cool.

Child: It is cold.

Teacher: Yes, when it is very cold, many of us will wear a hat and mittens. I will write *very cold* on this strip of paper and attach a hat-and-mittens marker to it. What marker should we attach to our graph today?

For During the Month

Once a week focus on the accumulating data on the picture graph. You might ask questions similar to these:

Counting, Comparing, Analyzing Data To develop counting and comparing:

- What kind of clothing have we had most often? How did you figure that out?
- How many times have we graphed clothing for warm days so far?
- Is there any kind of clothing we haven't graphed?
- Does our sample show more cool days or warm days? How many more? How do you know?
- How many Markers are shown on the Graph?
- Does the Graph show all the days in November to this day?
- What does this graph tell you?

Point out that weekend days are not included and that the month of November has more days in it than the number of days reported on the Graph.

"How many times have we graphed clothing for warm days so far?"

HELPFUL HINT

- While we have presented the Temperature/Clothing Graph as a picture graph, it could be done as a symbolic graph, if you prefer. Children can mark the Graph by pasting or pinning up colored paper squares, marking squares with an X, or shading in the squares with crayons. Plan on using the same format for the winter and spring Temperature/Clothing Graphs so the data from the different seasons can be easily compared.

ESTIMATION AND MEASUREMENT

Concepts & Skills

- Compare and order lengths
- Use the language of comparing
- Measure length using nonstandard units

Materials for November

4" × 12" pieces of construction paper in a variety of colors (one for each child); pen; straightedge; scissors; paper clips; a strip of butcher paper with tape added to the top for reinforcement (1 foot wide); paper bag

Author Notes

"This month children explore length by comparing the lengths of their shoes. Everyone has a chance to predict and discuss the outcome of matching up one shoe cutout with another. A bulletin board display is made with all the shoe cutouts arranged by length."

Setup

- On a 4" × 12" strip of construction paper, trace around the shoe of each child.
- Cut out the tracing and write the child's name on it.
- Place all the paper shoe cutouts in a paper bag.

Daily Routine

- Pull out two shoe cutouts from the bag each day. Read the names and invite those two children to come forward.
- Ask the class to look at their two classmates' shoe cutouts and predict the outcome when the cutouts are matched. Record the number of guesses for each of three possibilities (both are the same length, one is longer, or the other is longer) on the chalkboard.
- Have the two children examine the cutouts side by side and describe what they see, using words such as *same*, *longer*, or *shorter*.
- Finally, let the two children take their cutouts and decide where to hang them in the lineup from shortest to longest.

"Are any feet the same length?"

DISCUSSION

For Throughout the Month

Estimating, Comparing The following questions will spark discussion about the day's results.

- Were you surprised by the results when we matched up today's two cutouts? If you were, what surprised you?

- Was today's comparison hard or easy for our class to guess?
- Do you think the taller child will always have the longer foot? Are you certain?
- How many different lengths of feet do we have?
- Which is the shortest cutout? Which is the longest cutout?
- Do we have any feet the same length?

After the class has finished with the shoe cutouts collection, occasionally select two to three items from the classroom for the children to order from shortest to longest.

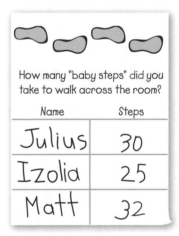

"Which one is longest?"

For the End of the Month

After all the children's cutouts have become a part of the display and the class has talked about the final outcome, take the set of cutouts down and place them in a basket. Let the children independently order the cutouts from shortest to longest. Invite children to try some of the activities described in Helpful Hints. As they investigate, ask questions such as:

- How can you be sure they are the same length?
- Which one did you think would be longer?
- What did you look at to help you decide?

HELPFUL HINTS

- If the shoe cutouts of the children seem to be too similar in length for comparison, collect a few shoe cutouts from other individuals in your school to include in this measurement activity.
- *Same as My Foot* Find your own cutout. Can you find some things in the room the same length as your foot?
- *Guess and Match* Choose any two cutouts. Guess if they are the same length or if one is longer. Match up the heels and find out.
- *How Many Steps?* With a friend, count your footsteps as you walk heel to toe across the room in a straight line. Write your name and how many steps it takes on a record sheet. At month's end, let children talk about what they have discovered. Look at the variety of answers for the footsteps across the room investigation. Why do they think the answers varied? Did lots of people count wrong or might there be another reason for getting different measurements? What if we all used the foot ruler? Would the counts come out the same then?
- It is easy to extend the comparing activities to include the use of nonstandard units. Near the foot cutouts place a container of square tiles or interlocking cubes that can serve as nonstandard units of length. Children can place them end to end down the center of their cutout and count them to determine a measure. You might want to add a collection of common objects, such as pencils, pens, pieces of yarn or string, paintbrushes, straws, and so on, for children to guess the length of and measure using the interlocking cubes.

How many "baby steps" did you take to walk across the room?

Name	Steps
Julius	30
Izolia	25
Matt	32

DECEMBER

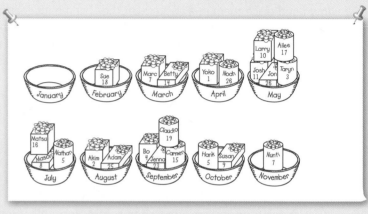

Estimation and Measurement

Every Day Calendar

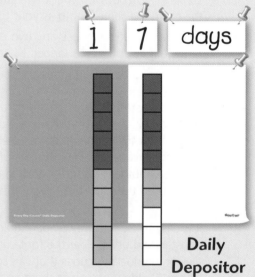

Birthday Baskets

Canned Food Graph

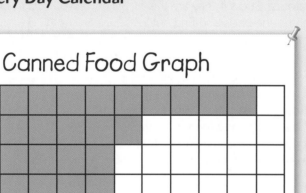

Soups										
Fruits										
Veggies										
Fish Meats										

Graph

1 7 days

Daily Depositor

55 56 57 58 59 60 61 62 63 64 65 66 67 68 69 70 71 72

Counting Tape

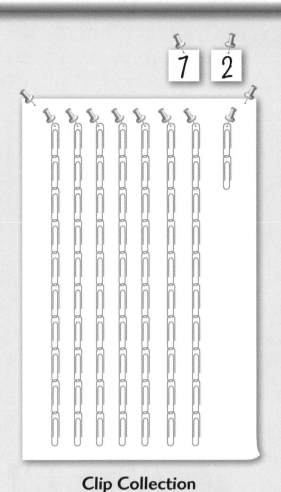

Clip Collection

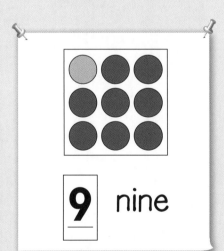

Domino Number Builder

December Elements

During December, it is often hectic as we try to accomplish a great deal before the school break arrives. To minimize teacher preparation, there are no new elements introduced this month. With the exception of the Graph, all the elements are used in ways similar to how they were used in September through November.

You will notice that the December holidays do not play a part in Calendar Math, since views differ widely on the role holidays should play in schools. If your school is one in which these holidays are incorporated into the classroom, you might want to adapt the Calendar to reflect them.

CALENDAR

Concepts & Skills

- Know the days of the week and names of the months
- Develop number sense
- Count on and count back
- Read, compare, and order numbers 1 to 31
- Recognize, analyze, and extend patterns
- Solve problems and use mental math
- Recognize that all triangles have three sides and three corners

Ongoing Assessment

1. How many red triangles do we have so far?
2. What is the same about all of the red triangles?
3. What color comes after the red triangle in this pattern?

Author Notes

"Most kindergarten children have a mental image of the triangle as an isosceles triangle (with two sides equal). The variety of triangles in this pattern (scalene, isosceles and equilateral) stimulates discussion about the shape and its characteristics. Children may be surprised to hear that there are different kinds of triangles. Explain that any closed shape with three straight sides is a triangle."

Daily Routine

- Each time a triangle appears on the day's Calendar Piece, ask questions to encourage children to comment on the variety of triangles they see.
- Occasionally chant the names of the months in order. Emphasize that December is the 12th and last month of the year.

DISCUSSION

For the First Day

Months of the Year Chant the names of the months in order, beginning with January, then repeat and have the children clap with you as you say *December*. Explain that December is the 12th and last month of the year. After reminding children of the number for the current year, ask them to predict the number for the new year.

Three-dimensional Shapes, Comparing Have children identify the December Birthday Basket and place it near the Calendar. Help children compare the numbers of different birthday present shapes they have seen in the Birthday Baskets this year from September through December. Some questions to encourage this kind of discussion and develop the language of comparing follow.

- Which of this year's Baskets has the most presents? The most box-shaped presents? The most cylinders?
- Which of this year's Baskets has the fewest cylinders? The fewest boxes? The fewest tall boxes?
- Which month does not have any tall boxes? Any flat boxes? Any cylinders?

The December Calendar Pieces create an ABB pattern using three different red triangles and a blue square rectangle.

- Does December have more presents than _____? How many more? How did you figure this out?

- Are there fewer presents in December than_____? How many fewer? How did you figure this out?

Allow children to arrange the December Present Pictures in order. Then have volunteers place them on the Calendar and share how they made their predictions. If you have chosen to recognize summer birthdays on those children's half-year "unbirthdays," place the June Basket near the Calendar as well. Ask children to predict where June Present Pictures will appear on the Calendar and attach the pieces. For additional questions see the discussions in October, page 33.

For the Second Week

Two-dimensional Shapes, Patterns, Counting Point out that a new pattern is beginning to appear on the December Calendar. Revisit October's Calendar for sample discussion questions. (See page 33.) Some additional ideas to encourage this discussion follow. We are referring to the square as a square rectangle. Determine the language that is most appropriate for your children.

- How many triangles do we have so far? How many squares (square rectangles)?

- Do we have more triangles or more squares (square rectangles)?

- What color do you think will come up next? What shape will it be? How many sides will it have?

- What do you notice that keeps happening over and over in this pattern?

- What color comes after the red triangle in this pattern? Does this always happen?

- What is the same about all of the red triangles? (There are three straight sides and three corners).

For Just Prior to December Vacation

Problem Solving The break for vacation offers a special opportunity for children to use their evolving understanding of patterns to predict the rest of the month's Calendar Pieces. Point to the space on the Calendar for the last day of the month and explain that it is also the last day of the year. Ask children:

- How many days until the year ends?

- What color piece do you think we will put here on the last day of the year?

Allow time for children to show on the Calendar how they figured out their predictions. Let children predict and put up the colored pieces for other December days until all of the month's pieces are up. Discuss where the new month will begin.

Patterns Then have children share their observations about the Calendar as they have done in the past. Some observations may include:

- There are more blues than reds.

- The pattern is one red, two blues, one red, two blues.

- The reds go down like stairs.

- The pattern goes ABBABBABB.

Susan: "There are more blues than reds."

Bo: "The blues come in twos after red."

Carmen: "The pattern goes 1 red then 2 blues, 1 red then 2 blues.

HELPFUL HINT

- Children may enjoy keeping track of the number of days left in the year. They could make a paper chain with the same color pattern as the Calendar, with each link representing one day left in the year. Place the chain near the Calendar. Each day remove one link from the chain. The remaining links could be counted each day. Before the break, children could make their own paper chains to take home for the countdown.

End-of-the-Year Countdown Chain

| Number & Operations | Algebra | Geometry | Measurement | Data & Probability |
| Problem Solving | Reasoning | Communication | Connections | Representation |

DAILY DEPOSITOR

Concepts & Skills

- Count with one-to-one correspondence
- Match quantities and numerals
- Compare quantities to 31
- Read numerals to 31
- Group and count by tens

Materials for December

Four 1" × 10" paper strips divided into ten units (TR14); a blue and a red crayon; tape or pins

Author Notes

"This month's Daily Depositor uses blank paper strips of ten units which are colored in, one unit per day. The first ten-unit strip is attached to the ones side of the Depositor. The first five units are colored blue, then the second five are colored red. This makes it easier to see the number of units at a glance. On the tenth day when the strip has been completely colored in, it will be moved to the tens side of the Depositor. The numerals are recorded above the respective mats. The children are continually verifying that the numerals match the quantity in the Depositor. Prior to leaving for December break, the class will predict the number of days left in the month (and year) and color them in.

Daily Routine

- On the first of December, attach a blank ten-strip to the ones side of the Depositor. Have a volunteer color the top unit blue.
- Record a *1* above the ones place on the Depositor record. Continue with the same procedure through the fifth of the month.
- On Mondays, color in units for Saturday, Sunday, and Monday, so the total is always the same as the day's date.
- On the sixth through the tenth, have the volunteer use a red crayon.
- On the tenth day, move the ten-strip to the tens side.

Ongoing Assessment

1. How many strips of ten have we colored so far?
2. How many squares have been colored so far?
3. How many squares are left to color on this strip? How did you get your answer?

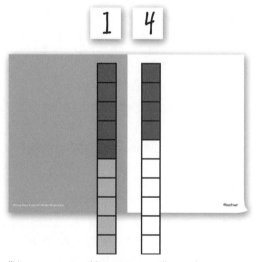

"How many more blue squares will we color on this strip?"

- On the 11th, put up another blank strip on the ones side and continue the pattern of updating established in the first ten days.

- Each day have the class tell how many tens they see and how many extra ones they see as you record the tens and ones digits.

Discussion

For Throughout the Month
Sample Dialogue

Teacher: How many units have been colored in so far on our strips?

Class: Fourteen have been colored in.

Teacher: Yes, 14. How did you know we had 14?

Child: There's 1, 2, 3, 4, . . . , 14.

Teacher: Yes, that's correct. We have 1 full strip of ten and 4 more. We can get to 14 by beginning at 10.

Teacher & Class: Ten, . . . , 11, 12, 13, 14.

Teacher: Let me record that. I'll write a *1* for the 1 group of ten above the tens and a *4* for the extra ones above the ones. Let's read it together.

Teacher & Class: One group of ten and 4 make 14.

Teacher: How many more days will be colored in blue on the new strip and how can you be sure?

Child: One more. That will be 5. Then we will start using red.

Teacher: That's true. How many more days until we complete the strip of ten?

Child: We will complete it in 6 more days.

Teacher: Yes. The 4 we have and 6 more will make 10. What day of the month will this be? Will we still be in school or on our break?

For the Last Day Before Break

Addition and Subtraction Concepts, Problem Solving On the last day before break, put up the remaining ten-strips and one extra unit to show a total of 31 units. Explain that these 31 units represent all the days in December. Some of the following questions may help to elicit problem-solving strategies.

- How many days have been colored in so far? How can you prove this?

- How many blank squares or units are left to be colored in this month? How did you get your answer?

- Did you count all the blank units or did you use a shortcut? If you used a shortcut, could you share it with us?

- The blank units are the days that are left in December, the last month of the year. December 31 will be the last day of the year. So how many days are left in this year?

- Tomorrow, how many days will be left? On December 30, how many days will be left?

"How many days until the end of the year?"

HELPFUL HINTS

- The children might enjoy making their own End-of-the-Year Countdown Tapes by taping 3 ten-strips and 1 extra unit together. Color in units up to the present day of the month. Then they can keep track of the days left until the New Year.

- You might suggest to parents that the completed strip be used as a track for a marker game in which players take turns telling what space they are on and tossing a dotted number cube or drawing a number card from a bag to determine the spaces to move their markers ahead. The first to go off the end of the track wins. The children might also use the completed strip to measure things in the home, searching for things that are 5 units, 10 units, or 30 units long.

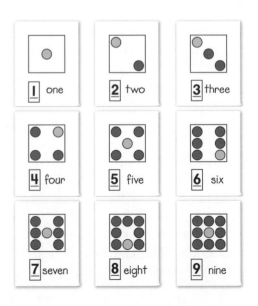

New Year's Countdown Tape Game

Number & Operations   Algebra   Geometry   Measurement   Data & Probability
Problem Solving   Reasoning   Communication   Connections   Representation

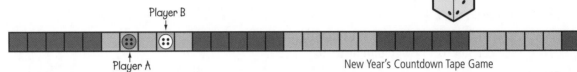

DOMINO NUMBER BUILDER

Concepts & Skills

- See quantities as one more than another quantity
- Count with one-to-one correspondence
- Compare and order quantities to 9
- Match quantities and numerals
- See sets of 2 through 9 as combinations of smaller sets

Ongoing Assessment

1. How many more dots do we have today than yesterday?

2. If I cover up one dot how many dots still show?

3. Can you tell me a story for today's Domino?

Materials for December

9 Domino Records (TR7); black, blue, and red markers; 0–9 Digit Cards (TR3); 9 paper clips

Author Notes

"This month's Domino dots are filled in with two colors to illustrate combinations of sets. The increasing quantities are shown as 1 red dot and a growing number of blue dots. At this time, it is important for children to see and talk about number relationships without writing number sentences. Understanding "one more" and "one less" will help children when they are ready to add and subtract."

Daily Routine

- Outline dots on a Domino Record (TR7) for each of nine days. This month, have a volunteer color in one outlined dot red and then color the remaining dots for the day blue.

- Each day discuss the relationship between the number of blue dots and the total number of dots.

DISCUSSION

For Early in the Month

Present the idea *one more than* with a discussion similar to this one.

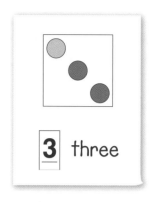

3 three

3 is 1 more than 2.

Sample Dialogue

Teacher: Does anyone remember what Domino we colored yesterday?

Child: I do. We colored 2 dots.

Teacher: Good. I will outline 3 circles in a diagonal on the Domino today. We will color 1 dot red and the other 2 dots blue. Here's my story: I had 2 pennies and I got 1 more. Now I have 3. Would anyone else like to share a story about three?

Child: I would. I have 3 goldfish.

Teacher: Great! Now can anyone tell a story about 2 and 1 more, just like our Domino shows?

Child: We had 2 kids and our new baby is 1 more.

Teacher: (holding the Domino for 2 next to the Domino for 3) How is the Domino for 3 different from the Domino for 2?

Child: Three has 1 more dot.

Teacher: That is absolutely true. I am going to write the sentence *3 is 1 more than 2* under our Domino picture for today.

As conversations like this continue throughout the month, children will begin to see the pattern that each number is 1 more than the number before it. Some questions like the following might be asked.

Addition and Subtraction Concepts To develop an understanding of number relationships:

- How many more dots do we have today than yesterday?

- If we compare the dots for 4 and 5, which has more? (holding up Dominoes for 4 and 5)

- If I cover up one dot, how many will we have?

- (on day 4 of coloring Dominoes) Who has a story for 3 and 1? (on day 7 of coloring) Who has a story for 6 and 1?

- Does the story match our Domino for today?

- Today we colored the Domino for 7. How many more to get to 9?

- (On day 6 of coloring Dominoes) What will we add to 6 to get to 7?

For After Coloring Nine Dominoes

Problem Solving After nine days, all of the Dominoes will be colored. Try some of the activities detailed in Helpful Hints to extend children's understanding of one more than a quantity. Encourage children to share their thinking with such questions as:

- How did you figure this out?

- How did you get your answer?

- Did anyone else get an answer a different way?

HELPFUL HINTS

- *Guess What I've Got* Hold a certain number of counters in your hand. Tell a riddle, "I've got 1 more than 3 counters. How many do I have?" After a few days of playing with the whole class, children can play the game together.

- *Can You Find It?* Use the Counting Tape to encourage children to see number relationships. Ask such things as, "I am looking for a number on the Counting Tape that is 1 more than 7. What color is it? What number is it? I am looking for a number on the Counting Tape that is 1 less than 5. It is on a blue square. What number am I looking for?"

Number & Operations	Algebra	Geometry	Measurement	Data & Probability
Problem Solving	Reasoning	Communication	Connections	Representation

COUNTING TAPE AND CLIP COLLECTION

Concepts & Skills

- Develop number sense
- Count with one-to-one correspondence
- Count and group by tens and ones
- Match quantities with numerals
- Compare and order quantities
- Count on and count back
- Discover number patterns and use mental math
- Solve problems

Ongoing Assessment

1. What are the number neighbors for 53?
2. How many clips have we added to our Collection since Day 60?
3. How many more days are there until Day 70?

Daily Routine

- Update daily.
- Introduce the phrase "number neighbors" to describe numbers that are adjacent to each other on the Counting Tape.
- Ask questions that relate number patterns to color patterns.
- Introduce and occasionally play the game *I'm Thinking of a Number.* (See Helpful Hint.)

DISCUSSION

51 52 73 54 55 56 57 58 59 60 61 62 63

"What color is the square we put up 10 days ago?"

For During the Month

Addition and Subtraction Concepts Introduce the term "number neighbor" to refer to a number that is found "next door to" another number. Continue to ask children questions like the following that involve comparing numbers, counting on, counting back, and counting by tens and ones. Remind children that patterns on the Clip Collection or Counting Tape can help them find answers.

- What would 63 and 1 more day be?
- What are the number neighbors for 63? (62 is 1 less and 64 is 1 more.)
- Which number is less, 50 or 63? Why? Let's start at 50 and count on to today's date.

- How many more days are there until Day 65? Day 70?
- How did you decide that?
- What number is on the square that we put up 1 day ago? 5 days ago? 10 days ago? Can anyone share how you figured out your answers?
- How many squares have we put on our Tape since we put up number 60?
- How many completed chains will we have on Day 70?
- How many clips have we added to our Collection since Day 60?
- Today is Day 63. How many more clips do we need to add to get to 64?

Since many kindergarten children need repeated experiences with numbers 1–20, adapt any of the questions above as well as the Helpful Hint below, for the smaller numbers.

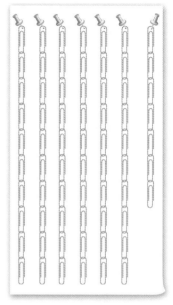

"How many clips did we have in our collection yesterday?"

Helpful Hint

- Children enjoy playing the game *I'm Thinking of a Number.* Give clues for a number on the Counting Tape, and have the children use the Tape or the Clip Collection to figure out the number. These clues provide different degrees of challenge for children.

  I'm thinking of a number that . . .

  is a neighbor number of 12.

  is 1 more than 15.

  is 2 more than 11.

  is between 17 and 19.

  is just after 22 and just before 24.

  is more than 33 and less than 35.

  is the same as 2 groups of 10.

  is the same as 4 groups of 10 and 1 more.

Number & Operations	Algebra	Geometry	Measurement	Data & Probability
Problem Solving	Reasoning	Communication	Connections	Representation

GRAPH

Concepts & Skills

- Collect and record data on a graph over time
- Read and interpret data on a picture or bar graph
- Count and compare quantities
- Sort and classify
- Make predictions

Materials For December

Every Day Graph (TR8), marking pen

Ongoing Assessment

1. How many cans have we collected so far? How did you decide?

2. If we were to put the cans in groups of ten, how many groups would we make? How many cans would be left?

3. How many cans do you think we will have by vacation? Why do you think so?

Author Notes

"Since many school communities are committed to canned food drives for charity at this time of year, we offer some suggestions for sorting and graphing such a collection."

Daily Routine

- After several cans have accumulated, have children sort the cans in several ways and then decide upon the categories for the Graph.
- Have children who have brought cans draw an X or color in the spaces so that all the cans collected so far are represented on the Graph.
- Have children who bring in cans on subsequent days mark them on the Graph before they add the food to the class collection.
- Once or twice a week focus discussion on the data on the graph.

Discussion

For the First Week

Following the children's suggestions, sort the cans several times. To get them started, ask children to look at the collection and offer one thing they notice about the cans. For example, one child may say that some cans are small and others are big, leading to sorting cans by size. Another might mention that some cans contain beans, resulting in sorting by content. After sorting many ways, the children can choose to graph the cans by the categories suggested by one of the sortings.

Sample Dialogue

Teacher: Let's look at all the cans that have been brought in so far. Who can tell us something about the cans?

Child: Two are soups.

Teacher: Yes, let's put all the cans of soup over here, and leave the cans that are not soup over there. Which do we have more of, soup or not soup?

Class: We have more that are not soup.

Teacher: Let's put the cans back together. Did anyone notice something else about the cans?

Child: Some have pictures of foods on them.

Teacher: Let's sort by pictures and no pictures. Which group has fewer cans?

Class: There are fewer with no pictures.

Teacher: We'll put the cans back together again. What else do you notice about the cans?

Child: They are different colors.

Teacher: Yes. Could you sort them by their colors? What should we do with this one that has both yellow and green on it?

Child: Don't count the picture on it, just the paper.

"How many cans have we collected so far?

"Who can tell us something you notice about these cans?"

Teacher:	We'll go by the main color on the label and not count the picture. How many different color groups do we have?
Class:	There are six groups.
Teacher:	Are there two groups that have the same number of cans?
Child:	The yellows and the whites both have 3 cans.
Teacher:	Let's put them together again. What else do you notice?
Child:	Green beans and corn are vegetables.
Teacher:	Let's put the vegetables together. How many vegetables do we have?
Child:	Five cans of vegetables. What about the chicken soup? It has some vegetables in it.
Teacher:	We may need a category for foods that have both vegetables and other items.

For Throughout the Month

Analyzing Data Once or twice a week focus discussion on the Graph. Ask some questions that involve children in analyzing data. For example:

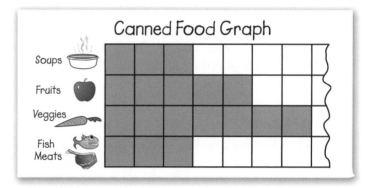

- What are some things we know from looking at our Graph?

- How many cans have we collected so far? How did you decide? Did someone else figure this out a different way?

- How many cans do you think we will have by vacation?

- What kinds of cans do we have the most of at this time?

- I see two groups that have the same number of cans. Which two groups are they?

- Do we have more cans of fruit of more cans of soup? How many more? (Let's "partner" the fruit and soup cans to see how many extra fruit cans we have.)

- How many more soup cans would we need to add so the soup row and the fruit row would have the same amount?

- If we were to put the cans in groups of ten, how many groups would we make? How many cans would be left?

"Which two groups have the same number of cans?"

Helpful Hint

- If you have access to a balance scale, this might be a good time to put it out with a few cans. Have the children choose two cans and, without looking at the labels, guess which one is heavier. Then have the children place the cans on the scale to check their guesses. (See Estimation and Measurement, page 70.)

Comparing the weights of two cans

ESTIMATION AND MEASUREMENT

Concepts & Skills

- Estimate and compare weights
- Use the language of comparing weights: *heavier, lighter, weighs more, weighs less, weighs the same*

Materials for December

A balance scale or a pair of teacher-made spring scales (see Helpful Hints); a collection of common objects with different shapes, sizes, and weights (for example, a can of tuna, a box of crayons, a hole punch, a chalkboard eraser, and a roll of tape)

Author Notes

"This month children explore weight by comparing the weights of different objects. Everyone has a chance to predict the outcome of matching up two objects on a balance scale and to talk about the results."

Daily Routine

- Two or three times a week, show the class two objects. Have children indicate which one they think is heavier or whether they think they weigh the same. Record the number of guesses for each outcome on the chalkboard.

- Pass the objects around so children can hold one in each hand. Let the class guess again to see if there is a change in the number of guesses after holding the objects.

- Have a volunteer place the objects on each side of the balance scale or into each of two side-by-side teacher-made spring scales so children can check their predictions.

- Use words such as *heavier* and *lighter*, or *weighs more*, *weighs less*, and *weighs the same* to describe the result of comparing the objects.

Ongoing Assessment

1. Do you think the chalk or the can of tuna is heavier?
2. What do you think might weigh the same as the roll of tape?
3. Which of these objects do you think might be lighter than the box of crayons?

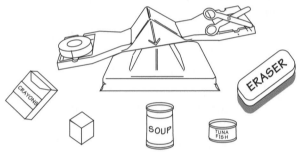

Checking the Estimate

DISCUSSION

For Throughout the Month

Occasionally focus on the day's guesses. Ask children to share why they guessed as they did. Have the class look at the number of children who made each guess, and discuss whether the weights of the objects were easy or hard to guess. Use a few of the following questions to spark further conversation.

Comparing, Estimating To develop the language of comparing weights, and practice making predictions about weight:

- Was anyone surprised by what happened when we put the objects on the scale?

- Would someone be willing to share their guess and discuss why that guess was made?
- Did you think the bigger object would be heavier this time?
- Did anyone try to think about what the objects are made of?
- Will the larger of two objects always be the heavier one?
- Did anyone think about having held similar objects before and how heavy they felt in your hands?
- Did anyone use past comparisons to help make a guess today? What did you remember?

To Sum Up

Ask children to think about all the objects that have been paired up on the scale and to guess which one weighs the most of all. Tally the guesses. Let children experiment and test their predictions, using the scale and objects over a few days. Finally, at month's end, let children talk about what they have discovered. Then compare the object that received the greatest number of guesses to each of the other objects using the balance scale. If a heavier object is found, use it instead to compare with the remaining objects. Is the heaviest object the one guessed by the most people or was it hard to predict?

HELPFUL HINTS

- One purpose of the daily estimation this month is to encourage children's natural interest in weighing and comparing things using scales. The demonstration activity is no substitute for hands-on exploration with a balance scale or spring scales during free time.

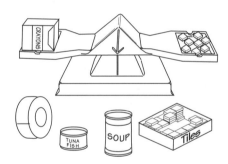

"The crayons weigh the same as 8 tiles."

- To protect the scale, make it a rule that only one item may be placed on a side. Limit the scale's use to one or possibly two children at a time. To ensure fair turns, some teachers have children cross their names off a class list after their turn and not return until everyone else who wants a turn has had a chance to use the scale.

- It is easy to extend the comparing activities to include the use of nonstandard units. Near the scales, place a container of ceramic tiles, large metal washers, or wooden cubes, which can serve as nonstandard units of weight. Children can place an object on one side of the scale and the nonstandard units on the other until both sides balance or nearly balance. Then the units can be taken out and counted. The results can be used to compare and order the objects by their weights.

- If you don't have access to a balance scale, you can make a pair of spring scales fairly easily. Punch four equidistant holes near the upper rim of a plastic margarine tub. Tie four strings to the tub using the holes. Pull all the strings up together and tie them in a knot centered 4 to 5 inches above the tub. Trim any excess string that is hanging beyond the knot. Finally, attach a rubber band at the knot in the way you would attach a luggage tag to a handle. Make a partner scale out of a matching margarine tub and an identical rubber band. The knots must each be at the same height. The scales can be attached by their rubber bands to two rulers, each anchored to a table by stacks of heavy books.

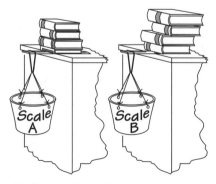

Teacher-made Spring Scales

JANUARY

Every Day Calendar

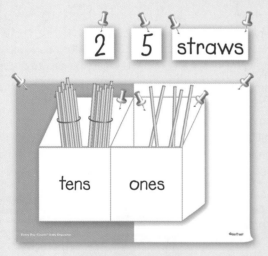

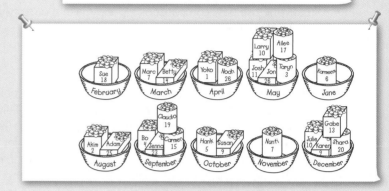

Birthday Baskets

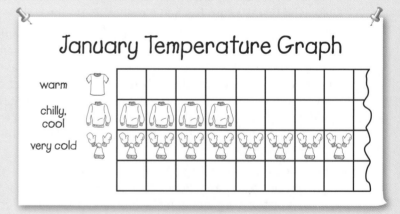

Estimation and Measurement

2 5 straws

tens ones

Daily Depositor

January Temperature Graph

warm

chilly, cool

very cold

Graph

69 70 71 72 73 74 75 76 77 78 79 80 81 82 83 84 85 86 87 88

    Counting Tape

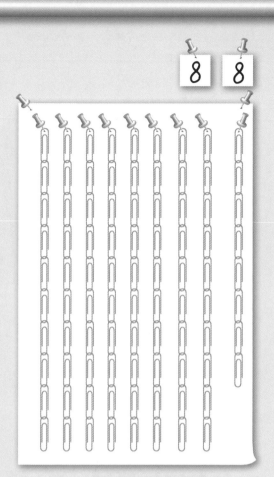

Clip Collection

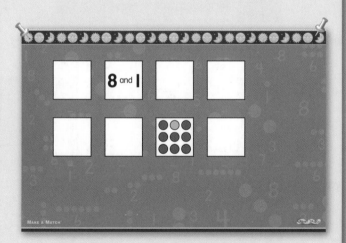

Domino Number Builder

In January the Calendar reveals a new pattern. The
Domino Number Builder emphasizes adding 2 onto
a quantity, and the Daily Depositor continues to
provide more experience with organizing and
comparing quantities to 31, using plastic straws
this month. Estimation and Measurement offers
experiences comparing the capacity of two
containers. For the Graph children collect winter
temperature data.

As Day 100 draws near, the Counting Tape and
the Clip Collection ask, "How many more until we
have 100?" It's time to get children to think about
what kind of collection of 100 objects they want
to gather and have ready by Day 100.

Number & Operations   Algebra   Geometry   Measurement   Data & Probability
Problem Solving   Reasoning   Communication   Connections   Representation

CALENDAR

Concepts & Skills

- Know the days of the week and months of the year
- Develop number sense
- Count with one-to-one correspondence
- Count on and count back
- Read, compare, and order numbers 1 to 31
- Recognize, analyze, and extend patterns
- Solve problems and use mental math
- Explore and describe the attributes of cylinders and rectangular solids

Ongoing Assessment

1. Can you find a Present Picture that has the same shape as today's Calendar Piece?

2. Which Calendar Pieces show a shape that can roll?

3. What is the same and what is different about today's Calendar Piece and yesterday's Calendar Piece?

Daily Routine

- Remind children that January is the first month of the year. Chant all twelve months together several times this month.
- This month, include the number of the year when reading the date.
- Add July "unbirthdays" to the Calendar this month, as well as January birthdays.
- Point out the variety of box shapes (rectangular solids) shown on the Calendar Pieces. Ask children to comment on the variety of boxes they see, to make generalizations about the boxes, and to compare the boxes to the cylinders.

DISCUSSION

For the First Day

When you return to school in January, attach Calendar Pieces with the help of the children up to the current day. This month each time a volunteer places the Today Arrow Marker above the day and reads the day's date, be sure he or she includes the number of the year as well as the month and the name and number of the day. Do the same with the Yesterday Arrow Marker.

Problem Solving Have children identify the January Basket and place it near the Calendar. Ask volunteers to arrange the Present Pictures in order and predict where each should be placed on the Calendar. If you are going to recognize summer birthday children on their "unbirthdays," repeat this activity with the July Birthday Basket and Present Pictures. A special Present Picture can be included to mark January 15, the birthday of Martin Luther King, Jr. Ask a volunteer to place the special piece on the Calendar.

Counting, Comparing To encourage comparing, problem solving, and mental math using the Birthday Data, see pages 28 and 33 for sample questions. In this month and the following one, it is easy to compare the number of winter birthdays to those in summer.

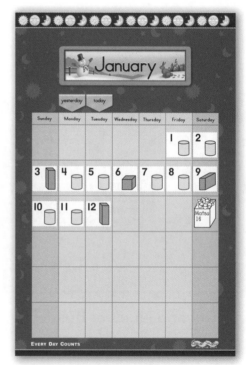

The January Calendar Pieces create an AAB pattern using two yellow cylinders followed by one of three different blue rectangular solids.

DISCUSSION

For the Second Week

Three-dimensional Shapes This month, invite children to make observations about the three-dimensional shapes on the Calendar Pieces. Questions such as the following will help them identify the attributes of the different shapes.

- What do you notice about all the yellow shapes?
- Do you see any birthday Present Pictures that are the same shape as the yellow shapes?
- What shape is on the top and the bottom of the yellow can shape?
- What do you notice that is the same about all the blue shapes?
- Do any of the birthday Present Pictures match this box?
- Can you find a box-shaped object in the room that looks like this cube-shaped box?
- What shape do you see on each face of a cube like this?

Algebraic Thinking Again ask children to suggest body motions to interpret this month's AAB pattern. For example, someone might suggest using feet to tap on A and stomp on B, creating a tap, tap, stomp sequence. Let children use connecting cubes to create the AAB pattern throughout the month. Continue to have children use various classroom materials to create their own patterns. Encourage them to use color, shape, size and texture when building their patterns.

To Sum Up

At the end of the month, ask children to share their observations about the January Calendar. Focus on language to describe the 3-D shapes as well as the various patterns that the children notice. Discuss where January ends and the new month, February, begins. Mark the day of the week where February will begin.

"There are more yellows than blues."

"The can shapes come in twos."

"I see 3 different kinds of boxes."

"The first box shape is like the shape of my Present Picture."

Number & Operations	Algebra	Geometry	Measurement	Data & Probability
Problem Solving	Reasoning	Communication	Connections	Representation

DAILY DEPOSITOR

Concepts & Skills

- Count with one-to-one correspondence
- Match quantities and numerals
- Compare quantities to 31
- Read numerals to 31
- Group and count by tens

Materials for January

31 coffee stirrers, craft sticks, or straws; 3 rubber bands; 2 Depositor Boxes labeled *tens* and *ones*; small paper bag

Ongoing Assessment

1. How many straws do we have in the ones box today?

2. How many more straws do we need to get ten straws?

3. We have 1 bundle of ten and 2 leftover ones. How should I write that number?

Author Notes

"The items collected in the Depositor vary from month to month in order to help children see the quantities 1 to 31 organized into tens and ones in different ways. This month coffee stirrers, craft sticks, or straws are collected and bundled into tens with rubber bands. Starting a fresh collection on the first of each month provides repeated opportunities for children to practice the counting sequence to 31 with one-to-one correspondence. It also provides opportunities for them to group and count objects by tens and ones and learn to read and write these numbers with understanding. The teen numbers, which sometimes cause confusion, are revisited each month. When children experience them as 1 group of ten and 1, 1 group of ten and 2, 1 group of ten and 3, and so on, it is easier to see how to write them without reversals."

Daily Depositor on January 16

Setup

- Clip the *ones* and *tens* Depositor Boxes to the Depositor Poster.

Daily Routine

- Each day have a child place one straw (coffee stirrer) in the box on the ones side of the Depositor. Record the total number of straws at the top of the Depositor.

- On Mondays, add two extra straws for Saturday and Sunday so the total in the Depositor is always the same as the day's date.

- Whenever 10 straws accumulate, bundle them with a rubber band and move the bundle to the box on the tens side of the Depositor.

- Announce the number of groups of ten and the number of ones as you record the numeral.

DISCUSSION

For the Middle of the Month
Sample Dialogue

Teacher: How many straws do we have in all today?

Class: We have 16.

Teacher: Yes, 16. How did you know we had 16?

Child: The number for yesterday was 15, so today has to be 16.

Teacher: Yes. Fifteen and one more is 16. How can we be sure?

Child: Count them.

Teacher: Will you show us how you would count them?

Child: Here's 10 in the rubber band and here's 11, 12, 13, 14, 15, 16.

Teacher: So you started with the 1 bundle of ten and counted on for the rest. Let's all try that.

Teacher & Class: 10, 11, 12, 13, 14, 15, 16.

Teacher: Let me record that. I'll write a *1* for the 1 group of ten above the tens box and a *6* for the loose ones above the ones box. Even though we hear the 6 first when we say 16, we don't write the 6 first. We need to write the 1 group of ten first and then the 6 last. Let's read the number together.

Teacher	
& Class:	1 group of ten and 6, 16.
Teacher:	If I take out 1 straw, how many will there be?
Class:	We will have 15.
Teacher:	Yes. If we have 16 today, how many straws will we have in 2 more days?
Child:	There will be 18.

For the End of the Month

Problem Solving, Counting, Comparing On the last day of the month, the 31 straws can be removed from the Depositor and used to introduce the two games described in Helpful Hints. The first involves looking for a pattern and using a strategy. The second is a counting and comparing game. Gather the class around you and invite a child to be your partner as you demonstrate for everyone to see.

HELPFUL HINTS

Pick Up Sticks Set out six straws. Take turns picking up either one or two straws each time. The child who takes the last straw wins. Play three or four times. Ask everyone whether they think it's best to have the first or second turn. Suggest they try out their ideas by playing the game at home using toothpicks or pennies. Maybe they can figure out a way to win every time. When they find the game predictable, suggest they start with seven or eight sticks. Can they use the same pattern to help them plan their moves to win?

Collect and Count Place the 31 straws on the floor in a pile. Select a Digit Card from a sack of 0 to 5 Digit Cards (TR3) and take this number of straws from the pile. Return the card to the sack. Let your partner select a card and take this number of straws from the pile. Continue taking turns, telling your partner your total each time before drawing the next card. Whenever one of you collects ten straws, group them in a pile of ten. The game ends when all the straws from the pile have been taken. Compare the totals. The person with more wins.

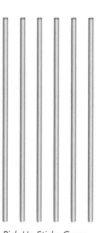

Pick Up Sticks Game

Number & Operations	Algebra	Geometry	Measurement	Data & Probability
Problem Solving	Reasoning	Communication	Connections	Representation

DOMINO NUMBER BUILDER

Concepts & Skills

- Count with one-to-one correspondence
- Visualize domino arrangements for 1 through 9
- Match quantities and numerals
- See sets from 1 to 9 as combinations of smaller sets
- Use spatial problem solving
- Understand and use position words

Ongoing Assessment

1. What do you see on this card?
2. What combination of numbers are you searching for?
3. Do you want to turn over the second card or the third card in this row?

Materials for January

1–9 Dotted Domino Halves (TR9); 2–9 Number Combination Cards (TR16); blue and red markers; Make a Match Poster

Author Notes

"This month the Domino Number Builder again becomes a Make a Match memory game, giving the children a chance to match small sets of blue and red dots with number combinations (such as 5 and 1) using Dominoes and Number Cards. Dominoes and Number Combination Cards for quantities 2–5 are explored first, followed by Dominoes and Number Combination Cards for quantities 6–9."

Setup

- Prepare the Domino Halves to match the large Domino Records created in December (see page 64).

Daily Routine

- The first day show the children the Dominoes and the Combination Number Cards for 2 though 5 that they will be matching. Then randomly place the cards onto the poster face-down in two rows of four cards.

- Have volunteers choose two cards at a time to turn over until a match is made. It may take several days until all matches are found.

- When all the matches for quantities 2–5 have been found, begin again with Domino Cards and Number Combination Cards for quantities 6–9.

"Four blue dots and one red dot matches 4 and 1."

Discussion

For Throughout the Month

A conversation similar to the following might occur the first time the game is played.

Sample Dialogue

Teacher: Today we are going to play Make a Match, our memory game with our Dominoes and the Number Cards. Let's look at our cards. What do you notice?

Child: Some are dominoes and some have numbers.

Child: And words.

Teacher: Let's read these cards that have words and numbers.

Teacher & Class: 1 and 1, 2 and 1, 3 and 1, 4 and 1, 5 and 1, 6 and 1, 7 and 1, 8 and 1.

Teacher: Do you see a domino that matches one of these number cards?

Child: That one that has 3 blue dots and 1 red one matches that card that says 3 and 1.

Teacher:	Yes, those two cards do match. Now I am going to place these cards facedown on the poster and then you get to search for Dominoes and the Number Cards that match. Who would like to be our first volunteer?
Child:	I want to turn over this one.
Teacher:	He is turning over the second card in the top row.
Child:	It's a Domino with 3 dots. Two are blue, and 1 is red.
Teacher:	Which card are you turning over next?
Child:	I will guess this one.
Teacher:	He turned over the first card in the bottom row. Is it a match?
Child:	No, it's 4 and 1.
Teacher:	What were you hoping to turn over?
Child:	I wanted to find 2 and 1.
Teacher:	Remember where these cards are placed. Let's turn them back over and try again for a match.

Helpful Hints

- Return random cards face-up to the poster. Ask for volunteers to tell stories, and invite the rest of the class to determine which card the story matches.

- Revisit questions that were asked in December. The class may also enjoy playing *Guess My Domino* again this month. (See page 51.)

Number & Operations   Algebra   Geometry   Measurement   Data & Probability
Problem Solving   Reasoning   Communication   Connections   Representation

COUNTING TAPE AND CLIP COLLECTION

Concepts & Skills

- Develop number sense
- Count and group by tens and ones
- Count on and count back
- Discover number patterns and use mental math
- Solve problems

Daily Routine

- Point out in discussions that the Counting Tape and Clip Collection are both getting closer and closer to 100.
- Begin preparations for a 100th day celebration in February.

DISCUSSION

For During the Month

Explain to the children that Day 100 will arrive soon. Ask volunteers to use the Counting Tape or the Clip Collection to find the number of days until Day 100. Let children share their strategies for finding their answers. You may want to create a countdown tape to Day 100 similar to December's countdown to the end of the year.

Ongoing Assessment

1. What number is one more than 70?
2. How many groups of ten do we have on the Clip Collection today?
3. If we take one chain of ten clips away, how many clips will be left on the board?

Number Sense To develop number sense by examining the relationship of one number to another, point to the number being featured and ask:

- How is number 63 different from 93?
- What is the same about 63 and 93?
- Which number is greater, 76 or 88? Why?
- Which number is 1 more than 28? Which is 1 less than 28?
- Find today's mystery number. Convince us of your answer using math talk. (It comes right after 35. It is a neighbor of 37. It has 3 groups of ten and 6 leftover ones.)

"What number is one more than 80?"

Place Value By the 80th day of school, children will have seen the counting sequence from 1 to 10 repeated eight times on the Counting Tape and Clip Collection. To promote understanding of grouping, ask:

- How many groups of ten do we have? How many leftover ones?
- Let's count on from our last group of tens.
- If we took away all of our leftover ones, how many clips would we have?

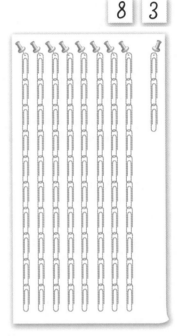

"How many more clips do we need to get 90?"

HELPFUL HINT

- Some teachers celebrate Day 100 by having children bring "Collections of 100" to school. Have children think about what they could collect. Make sure children know not to bring toys, money, or any collection they are particularly fond of. Parents are usually very willing to support such a project if given advance notice. Some items that have arrived on Day 100 include stickers, buttons, bread tags, old crayons, toothpicks, cotton balls, and macaroni of various shapes and sizes. Ask children to put their items into groups of tens so that everyone will be able to see the 10 groups of ten that make 100.

| Number & Operations | Algebra | Geometry | Measurement | Data & Probability |
| Problem Solving | Reasoning | Communication | Connections | Representation |

GRAPH

Concepts & Skills

- Collect and record data on a graph over time
- Read and interpret data on a picture or bar graph
- Count and compare quantities
- Understand temperature

Materials for January

Blank Every Day Graph (TR8), November Temperature Graph, Clothing Markers (TR13)

Ongoing Assessment

1. What does this Graph tell us?
2. Does our sample show more cool days or cold days? How many more? How do you know?
3. How many Markers are shown on the Graph?

Author Notes

"This month the Graph provides a record of clothing appropriate for temperatures in January. Graphing clothing again this month, as in November, allows the class to compare the local fall temperatures with the winter temperatures."

Daily Routine

- Each day have the class talk about the temperature outside and how it is reflected in what they would wear outside.
- Have a volunteer attach the appropriate Clothing Marker to the Graph.
- Discuss the accumulating data a few times each week.

"How many warm days do you think we will have in January?"

DISCUSSION

For the Beginning of the Month

As in previous months, consider letting children help you set up the Graph. Tell them you want to create a Graph that has the same headings in the same order as the November Graph so it will be easy to compare the data. With the November Graph in view, let them help you construct the new Graph.

Data Poll the class to have them determine which kind of clothing would be appropriate for the day's temperature. Ask children to raise their hand when you hold up the marker they think is best. Ask a volunteer to help you count the hands. Then place the marker selected by most children on the Graph. Looking at the November Graph, ask the class to indicate by a show of hands who thinks there will be more cool days in January than in November, fewer cool days, or the same. How about warm days? Tell the children they will compare the two temperature graphs at the end of the month.

For Later in the Month

Once a week focus on the accumulating data on the picture graph. You might ask some questions similar to these.

Number Sense To encourage counting and comparing:

- What kind of clothing have we had most often? How do you know?
- How many times have we graphed clothing for cool days?
- Is there any kind of clothing we haven't graphed?
- Does our sample show more cool days or cold days? How many more? How do you know?
- How many Markers are shown on the Graph?
- What does this Graph tell us?
- Did January have more warm days or fewer warm days than November?

Temperature Tally Graph

HELPFUL HINT

- While we have presented the Temperature/Clothing Graph as a picture graph, children could also keep a tally of the clothing worn.

ESTIMATION AND MEASUREMENT

Concepts & Skills

- Estimate and compare capacity
- Use the language of comparing capacity: *holds more, hold less, holds the same*

Materials for January

A dishpan of rice placed in a large shallow box; a funnel, dustpan, and whisk broom; a collection of unbreakable containers of different shapes and sizes labeled A, B, C, and so on

Author Notes

"This month children explore capacity by comparing the capacities of different containers. Invite volunteers to assist with the measuring. Give everyone a chance to predict the outcome of pouring one full container into an empty one and talk about the results. One intent of this month's measurement activity is to nurture children's natural interest in exploring capacity with containers. The demonstration activity is, of course, not a substitute for hands-on exploration at the sand or water table."

Daily Routine

- Choose at least two days each week to show the class one container that you have filled with rice and a second empty container of a different shape.
- Ask the class to predict what will happen when the rice in the full container is poured into the empty one. Record the number of guesses for each possibility on the chalkboard.
- Let a volunteer do the pouring, using a funnel when necessary.
- Discuss the outcome.

DISCUSSION

For Throughout the Month

Estimating Before pouring the rice, ask children to choose one of the following outcomes.

- Will the rice overflow?
- Will the rice just fill the second container?
- Will there be not enough rice to fill the second container?

Then, as time allows, talk about the results of the pour, using language such as *holds more, holds the same,* or *holds less.* Ask some of the following questions.

Ongoing Assessment

1. Which container do you think holds more?
2. Do you think the rice will overflow when I pour it into this cup?
3. Do you think it will always be the taller of the two containers that holds more?

Comparing To develop the language of comparing capacity and make predictions about capacity:

- Was anyone surprised by what happened?

- Would someone be willing to share your guess and discuss why you made that guess?

- Did the height, or tallness, of the container matter to you when you made your guess?

- Did you pay more attention to how fat, or wide, the container was?

- Did anyone think about both tallness and fatness?

- Were there other things you noticed about the containers that made you guess as you did?

- Do you think it will always be the taller of the two containers that holds more? Do you think a taller container can ever hold less than a shorter container?

Draw attention to the record of the guesses and ask if the day's prediction was easy or difficult to make. Did many children make a guess that matched what happened, or only a few?

For the End of the Month

Collecting Data Toward the end of the month, it is fun to have the class guess which of all the containers holds the most. Encourage children to think about some of the past comparisons before they make their guess. Tally the guesses. Let children experiment and test their predictions during activity periods for a few days.

Finally, at month's end, let children talk about what they have found out on their own. Consensus is rare! Then take the container that received the most guesses and compare it with each of the others in the collection. If a different container is found to hold more, use it to continue comparing the remaining containers. Is the container with the greatest capacity the one most people predicted or not? If not, why was it hard to tell it would hold the most?

HELPFUL HINTS

- It is easy to extend the comparing activities to include the use of nonstandard units. Simply add a small measuring scoop to the rice setup. During choosing times, children can tally the number of scoops required to fill the containers and use the results to make comparisons.

- Kitchen funnels do not work well with rice. You can cut off the top third of a plastic 2-liter soft-drink container, tape over the rough edge, and invert it to create an efficient funnel.

- If you use rice or another edible material, keep it in a container with a tight-fitting lid when it is not in use.

- Putting a large paper over the rice tub to indicate it is closed keeps hands out during class times when investigating the containers is not a choice.

Which do you think holds the most?

(Guesses)

Container B 𝄒𝄒𝄒𝄒 𝄒𝄒𝄒𝄒 𝄒𝄒 (12)

Container K 𝄒𝄒𝄒𝄒 (5)

Container C //// (4)

Container E 𝄒𝄒𝄒𝄒 // (7)

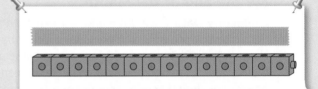

FEBRUARY

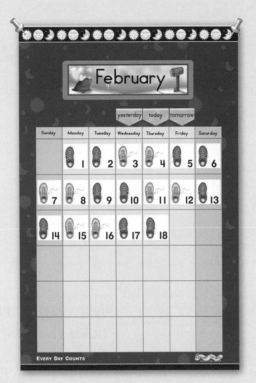

Every Day Calendar

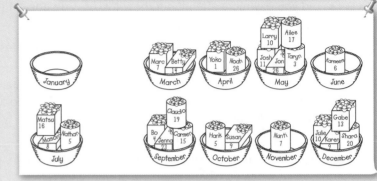

Birthday Baskets

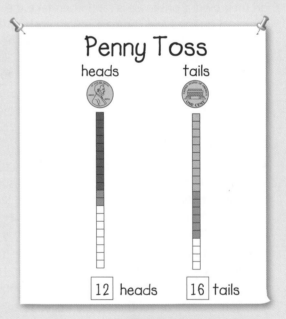

Estimation and Measurement

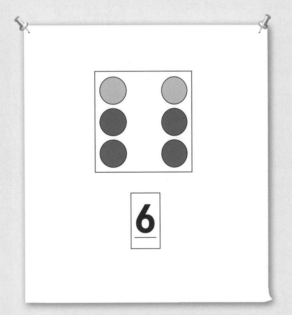

Domino Number Builder

Graph

Penny Toss

heads   tails

| 12 | heads | | 16 | tails |

88 89 90 91 92 93 94 95 96 97 98 99 100 101 102 103 104

 Counting Tape

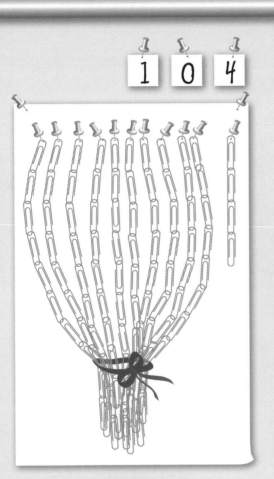

Clip Collection

Daily Depositor

FEBRUARY ELEMENTS

This month the Counting Tape and Clip Collection show Day 100 drawing near. The Calendar presents a new pattern of AABB, highlighting pairs of sneakers, and the Birthday Data incorporates Lincoln's and Washington's birthdays. The Domino Number Builder uses two red dots on each Domino to illustrate small sets made up of smaller ones. The Daily Depositor continues to help children organize and count, this time using tally marks. The Graph in February allows children to experience graphing the results of a daily penny toss to see how frequently the coin lands heads-up or tails-up.

CELEBRATING THE 100TH DAY OF SCHOOL

One hundred is a special number in our numeration system. For this reason, plan to set aside some time to do a few special activities on the 100th day of school. You might want to choose from the following suggestions or create several of your own.

Class Collection of 100 Objects Have children start a class collection of 100 items on Day 100. On each day, have children count to see how many objects they have collected. The collection could also be used for sorting activities.

100 Thumbprints Using 10 different colors, have children record 10 thumbprints in each color on a large piece of paper.

Big Book of 100 Ask children to complete the thought, "If I had 100. . ." Then have children draw a picture or write a story about their thoughts on a large piece of paper. Collect their ideas and make them into a big book the children can share and read.

Stringing 100 Along Have children string pieces of different colored macaroni together to make chains of 100 pieces. To color the macaroni, mix 3 teaspoons of alcohol and 10 drops of food coloring in a resealable plastic bag. Place the macaroni in the solution, shake for 15 seconds, then spread to dry on layered newspaper. You may want to knot the string after every ten pieces of macaroni to emphasize groups of ten.

What can we do in 100 seconds? It might be fun to count how many times children can clap their hands in a 100-second period. Other activities to count might include jumping jacks, steps around the room, times they can walk to the chalkboard, and circles they can make around their desks in 100 seconds. Allow children time to suggest additional activities to try in 100 seconds.

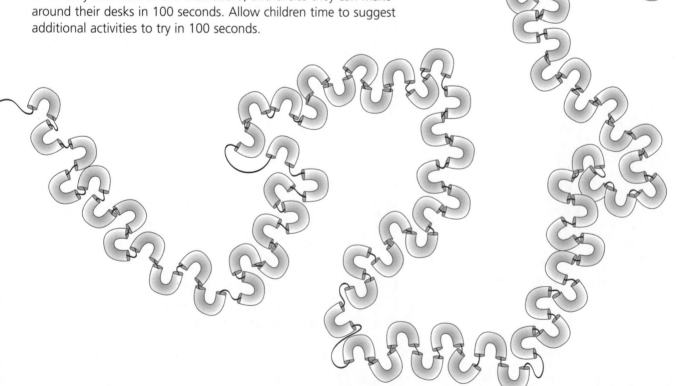

CALENDAR

Concepts & Skills

- Know the days of the week and months of the year
- Count on and count back
- Recognize, analyze, and extend patterns
- Identify a pair as a group of two
- Understand "tomorrow"

New Materials For the Year

Tomorrow Arrow Marker

Author Notes

"You might want to have two Present Pictures ready for the birthdays of Abraham Lincoln on February 12 and George Washington on February 22. Ask volunteers to place these pieces on the Calendar along with the class Present Pictures from February and August. If it is a leap year or if you have a child with a February 29 birthday, you might want to mention to children that February is unique among the year's months, since it gets an extra day every four years. Explain to the children why this happens."

Daily Routine

- Review the relationship between today and yesterday, then introduce the Tomorrow Arrow Marker.
- If you have decided to recognize "unbirthdays," remove the August Birthday Basket from the display and place it near the Calendar with February's.
- Use the pairs of sneakers on the Calendar to initiate discussions about pairs and everyday things that come in pairs.

DISCUSSION

For the First Day
Sample Dialogue

Teacher: What day is it today?

Class: Today is Thursday.

Teacher: Yes, and I will put the Today marker above Thursday. What day was it yesterday?

Class: Yesterday was Wednesday.

Teacher: Would anyone like to put up the Yesterday Marker? Can anyone tell me what day it will be tomorrow?

Class: Tomorrow will be Friday.

Teacher: That's right. I will put up the Tomorrow Marker above Friday.

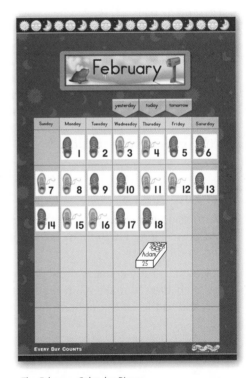

Ongoing Assessment

1. Can you show me where we will place our Calendar Piece tomorrow?

2. Does every shoe on the Calendar have a partner? How can you tell?

3. How many pairs of shoes are on the Calendar?

The February Calendar Pieces create an AABB pattern by using a par of tied red sneakers followed by a pair of untied yellow sneakers.

Analyzing Data, Comparing, Addition and Subtraction Concepts

Continue analyzing Birthday Data as in previous months (see pages 28 and 33). Point out that February is the second month of the year.

- Can you find two months that have four birthdays?
- Can you find two baskets that have the same number of birthdays and together have six?
- Can you find two months in which one basket has one more than the other? Two more than the other?

For the Second Week

Involve children in interpreting this month's pattern using body motions. Invite children to create the AABB pattern with connecting cubes. Ask the following questions to encourage discussion.

Number Sense To promote an understanding of pairs as grouping by twos:

- What do you notice about this month's pattern?
- Is there an extra shoe (one odd shoe without a mate)?
- When we add one more shoe tomorrow, do you think that each shoe will have a "partner" or will there be one extra shoe?
- When we had one pair of shoes, how many shoes did we have? Two pairs of shoes? Three pairs of shoes?
- How many pairs of shoes do we have on our Calendar?

To Sum Up

Patterns Near the end of the month, ask children to look at the Calendar and share with the class any patterns they see. You might want to record their observations and names in speech bubbles and attach them with a smaller version of the Calendar to a large piece of butcher paper or poster board.

HELPFUL HINTS

- At transition times or when lining up for library or lunch, some teachers fit in a few Birthday questions to entice children to combine sets and compare.
- Since the Calendar Pieces show pairs of shoes, it might be fun to invite children to make a list of other things that come in twos. You can add to the list throughout the month and even beyond.

"It goes two red shoes, two yellow shoes, two red shoes, two yellow shoes."

"There are always two tied shoes together and two untied shoes together."

"They are pairs."

"It goes AABBAABBAABB."

DAILY DEPOSITOR

Concepts & Skills

- Count with one-to-one correspondence
- Match quantities and numerals
- Group and count by tens
- Become familiar with tally marks

Materials For February

Four index cards or 3" × 6" pieces of white construction paper; the Depositor background; a wide-tipped marker

Author Notes

"This month tally marks will be collected on the Daily Depositor. When a card has been filled with 10 tally marks it will be moved from the ones side of the Depositor mat to the tens side. By using yet another model for place value exploration, the children have opportunities to generalize this concept of collecting objects in the special ones place and then grouping or moving them as ten to the special tens place."

Daily Routine

- Each day add a tally mark to the index card in the ones place.
- On Mondays, add tally marks for Saturday, Sunday, and Monday so the total number of tally marks is the same as the day's date.
- When you have 2 groups of five, move the card to the tens place.

DISCUSSION

For the Beginning of the Month

Introduce the tally as a way of keeping track of things being counted, such as the days of February. Let the children know that this month they will practice making tally marks by adding one mark each day. A discussion such as the following could occur on the fifth day.

Sample Dialogue

Teacher: Today is February 5th. How many tally marks do we need?

Class: Five.

Teacher: That's correct. So far, we have been making straight lines for our four tally marks. For our fifth line, we are going to make a slanted line (diagonal line). Let's count the lines: 1, 2, 3, 4, and our slanted line make 5. Whenever you see a group of tally marks like this, how many are there?

Class: Five.

Teacher: Let's practice making tally marks in the air.

Ongoing Assessment

1. We are on day 14. How many more to get to 15? 16?

2. If we took all of these tally marks on the ones side away, how many would be left just on the tens side of our Depositor?

3. How many tally marks will we have on the ones side tomorrow?

Tally marks show Day 5.

For Throughout the Month

Counting, Place Value To encourage children to use a variety of ways to count and group tally marks, ask questions such as the following.

- Is 14 more or less than 10? How do you know?
- Convince us that this is 14.
- What if we took all of these tally marks on the ones side away, how many would be left on the tens side of our Depositor? (Okay, so 14 take away 4 leaves us with 10.)
- We are on Day 14. How many more to get to 15? 16?
- Let's count on from 14 to 20. (Fourteen, 15, 16, 17, 18, 19, 20)

HELPFUL HINTS

- Some teachers choose to represent the tally marks with puff paint, or pretzels or craft sticks glued to the construction paper or index card.
- After the children have had experience with the tally, you may choose to represent some of your class surveys with tally marks.

Tally marks show Day 14.

Number & Operations	Algebra	Geometry	Measurement	Data & Probability
Problem Solving	Reasoning	Communication	Connections	Representation

DOMINO NUMBER BUILDER

Concepts & Skills

- See quantities as 2 more than another quantity
- Count with one-to-one correspondence
- Compare and order quantities to 9
- Visualize domino arrangements for 2 through 9
- See sets of 2 through 9 as combinations of smaller sets

Daily Routine

- Outline dots on a Domino Record (TR7) for each of eight days. This month, have volunteers color two dots red and then color the remaining outlined dots blue.
- Discuss the relationship between the number of blue dots and the total number of dots.

Ongoing Assessment

1. Can you tell me a story about 4 and 2 more?
2. Can you tell me a story to match what you see on this Domino?
3. If we color two dots red on this Domino, how many will we have left to color blue?

DISCUSSION

For Early in the Month
Sample Dialogue

Teacher: Today, I have circled 5 dots. We are going to color 2 red. How many will we color blue?

Child: I think there will be 3.

Teacher: How did you figure that out?

Child: I took 2 dots off the corners and that left 3.

Teacher: You mean you pretended 2 of the dots on the corners were red and that left 3 to be blue. Anyone else?

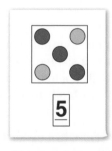

"5 is 2 more than 3."

Child:	I got 2 because 2 and 3 make 5.
Teacher:	I've got a story. "Three kindergartners were on the playground and two more came to play. Then there were five children." Would anyone like to share another story?
Child:	I would. I had 3 apples. I found 2 more. That makes 5 apples.
Teacher:	That's a wonderful story. Five is two more than three. Does anyone have another story?

After Coloring Eight Dominoes

After all of the Domino Records are filled in, continue to share the following ideas with the children, holding up the Dominoes being discussed.

Counting, Comparing To encourage comparing, and counting on, and to provide experiences telling story problems:

- We see 4 dots on this domino. How many more to get to 6?
- With 6 dots, how many more to get to 8?
- Does anyone have a story about 4 and 2 more?

Problem Solving, Algebraic Thinking The activities in Helpful Hints will give children additional experience seeing quantities as 1 more than and 2 more than another number.

As children work, ask questions to encourage them to verbalize their thought processes.

- How did you figure that out?
- Is there another way to figure that out?
- Can you think of a story to tell about that Domino?

HELPFUL HINTS

- *Find My Card* Spread out all of the Domino Cards that have 1 or 2 dots colored red. Give the children hints to find the Domino Card you are thinking about. For example, "I'm thinking of a Domino Card that shows 3 and 2 more. Who can find the card I am thinking about?"
- *Two-More-Than Designs* Using pattern blocks or connecting cubes, children create designs for each of the numbers 2 to 9. For example, for 5, children may choose to use 3 triangles and 2 squares or 3 yellow cubes and 2 orange cubes.
- Many teachers like to make big books to hold the Domino Records created for each number. Use 22" × 28" tagboard with holes punched along the side so that you can insert rings to flip the pages easily. On each page, write large numbers and attach the Domino Records (TR7) colored in thus far for that number.

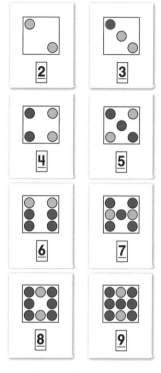

On eight days this month color 2 dots red and the others blue.

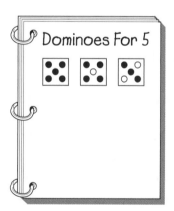

COUNTING TAPE AND CLIP COLLECTION

Concepts & Skills

- Count with one-to-one correspondence
- Count and group by tens and ones
- Match quantities with numerals
- Compare and order quantities
- Count on and count back
- Discover number patterns and use mental math

Materials for February

Ten-inch ribbon or string

Daily Routine

- Repeat the same sequence of colors used for each decade before Day 100 when putting up squares for Day 101 and all days thereafter.
- As time allows, have the class consider how many days left until Day 100, or how many days since Day 100.

| 86 | 87 | 88 | 89 | 90 | 91 | 92 | 93 | 94 | 95 | 96 | 97 | 98 | 99 | 100 |

DISCUSSION

"How many groups of ten do we have?"

For Early in the Month

Continue to ask the question, "How many more days until Day 100?" and have volunteers share their ways of answering this question. If you began a Countdown Strip last month, continue using it to help children see the number of days left until Day 100.

For the 100th Day of School
Sample Dialogue

Teacher: Let's look at yesterday's square. How many days have we been in school before today?

Class: We have been here 99 days.

Teacher: Yes. What comes after Day 99?

Class: Day 100 comes after Day 99.

Teacher: Yes 99 and 1 more is 100. What color do you think our square will be today?

Class: It will be white.

Teacher: Yes, the color of the square is white and the numeral is 100. Can someone tell me how many different colors we have?

Class: We have 10 colors.

Teacher: Yes, there are 10 colors, and the last one is white. Let's look at the Tape again. How many groups of ten do we have?

Class: We have 10 groups of 10 different colors.

Teacher:	Let's look at our Clip Collection. Can anyone tell me what will happen to the chain today when we add today's clip?		

Teacher: Let's look at our Clip Collection. Can anyone tell me what will happen to the chain today when we add today's clip?

Class: It will have 10.

Teacher: Yes, the chain will have ten clips and will be completed. How many chains of ten will we have today? Let's count together.

Teacher & Class: 1, 2, 3, 4, 5, 6, 7, 8, 9, 10.

Teacher: Yes, we have ten chains. Now let's count the number of clips that we have. Can anyone tell me how many we should have?

Class: We should have 100.

Teacher: Let's count them by tens together.

Teacher & Class: 10, 20, 30, 40, 50, 60, 70, 80, 90, 100.

Teacher: Yes, we have 100 clips, and these same 100 clips are made of ten chains of ten clips. What do you think the next number will be?

Child: It will be 200.

Child: It'll be a million.

Child: It will be 110.

Child: No, it will be 101.

Teacher: Keep thinking about it. We'll find out tomorrow.

On Day 100, tie the 10 chains of ten paper clips with a bow to show the group of 100. This helps children continue to see that 100 is made up of 10 groups of ten.

For Day 101 and Thereafter

Place Value On Day 101, ask children to predict the color of the square to put on the Tape. Before asking, have children repeat counting 10 groups of ten different-colored squares. Emphasize that 10 groups of ten makes 100. When 1 day is added to Day 100, some children will be surprised to find out that 101 follows 100. Use the Clip Collection to help them see that 101 follows 100. Ask:

- How many clips did we have when we had 80 clips and 1 more?
- How many clips did we have when we had 90 clips and 1 more?
- How many clips are in the Collection before we add today's clip?
- Now, after we added today's clip, how many clips do we have?

Emphasize that 100 and 1 left over is 101. Discuss numbers that appear on the following days in the same way. It won't be long before many see a familiar pattern unfolding in the numbers above 100.

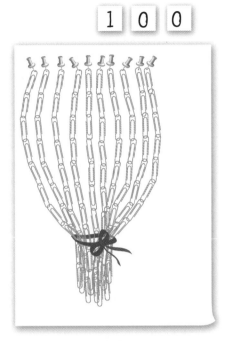

"What do you think the next number will be?"

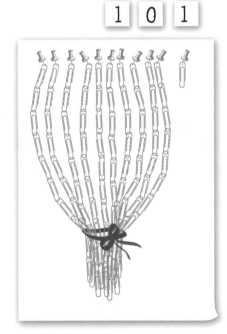

The Clip Collection shows that 100 and 1 left over is 101.

HELPFUL HINTS

- If you have been attaching the white dot stickers to the zeros in 10, 20, . . . , 90, and decorating them with the face of Zero the Hero, you'll want to make a special event of his appearing twice on Day 100. You may also wish to celebrate Zero the Hero Week since he keeps reappearing for ten more days. This is a great opportunity for building understanding of counting by ones beyond 100 and for reading and writing these numbers.

- Some teachers have arranged to have Zero the Hero visit on Day 100. Wearing a bright yellow cape decorated with the word Zero and the multiples of 10, Zero the Hero sweeps into classrooms, wanting to hear about the day's special events, and leaves behind zero-shaped cereal treats for everyone.

Zero the Hero appears for 11 days in a row.

- If you use flip cards with the Clip Collection you will need another set of them, with digits 0–9 for the hundreds place. Although the hundreds digit will not change throughout the school year, children will become familiar with seeing three digit numbers and matching quantities to these larger numbers.

- On Day 100, have children use a length of 100 clips to search for objects in the classroom that have the same length. Have them share what they have discovered and list the objects on a large piece of paper.

- Continue to have children search for a mystery number. Cover up a number with a blank square and ask the children to "guess" the hidden number, convincing the class of their selection. (I know that the mystery number is 52 because it comes right after 51. I know that it comes between 51 and 53. It is one less than 53).

- After Day 100, some teachers use two colors of paper clips grouped in chunks of fives to encourage the children to count on from 5.

| Number & Operations | | Algebra | Geometry | | Measurement | | Data & Probability |
| Problem Solving | | Reasoning | | Communication | | Connections | Representation |

GRAPH

Concepts & Skills

- Collect and record data from a probability experiment
- Analyze the results of a penny toss to predict chances
- Count and compare quantities
- Recognize both sides of a penny

Materials for February

Penny Demonstration Coin cardstock showing the heads and tails sides of the penny; two sheets of Inch Squares (TR14); two different-colored crayons; a penny

Ongoing Assessment

1. How many tosses have landed heads-up?
2. Do we have more heads or tails?
3. How many tosses have we made altogether?

Author Notes

"The penny toss provides an opportunity for children to become familiar with a penny and identify it by color, heads, or tails. Getting to know the penny in this way may help children recognize it easily and not confuse it with a nickel, which they will use in a future month. Introducing the one-to-one correspondence between pennies and cents may help children later in the month when they translate the number of heads and tails on the Graph into cents. In addition, children are exposed to the likelihood of getting heads or tails and graphing the results."

Setup

- Cut a sheet of Inch Squares (TR14) into strips of 10 squares.
- Use the strips to create a bar graph with two bars, one titled *heads* and one titled *tails*.

Daily Routine

- Each day assign two volunteers to the penny toss.
- Have one partner toss the coin twice as the other records each toss by marking a space on the heads or tails graphing grid.
- When one strip of ten squares is colored in, put up another one.
- Shade each strip differently to help children count more easily by tens and ones.
- Occasionally discuss the accumulating data.

DISCUSSION

For the First Day

Display the Demonstration Coin showing both sides of the penny and pass out a real penny to the class. Ask children to look at the picture and the coin in their hands and talk about what they see. Their observations will give you some openings to interject information about President Lincoln, the Lincoln Memorial, and the coin. Introduce the penny, its value, and the penny toss experiment in a discussion similar to the following.

Sample Dialogue

Teacher: What do you notice about the penny?

Child: It's brownish.

Teacher: Pennies are covered with copper metal, which gives pennies an orange-brown color. What else do you see?

Child: One side has a face.

Teacher: Yes, one side shows a face. Can anyone tell me who the person is on the penny?

Child: I think it is Lincoln.

Teacher: Yes, it is Abraham Lincoln. He was President over 125 years ago. We call the side with the face on it heads. Can anyone tell me what is on the other side?

Child: It's a building. **MORE ▶**

Penny Toss

heads   tails

6 heads   4 tails

"Do we have more heads or tails?"

Teacher:	That's right. This building is in Washington, D.C., and was built to honor President Lincoln and his ideas. We call this side of the coin tails. Let's look at the tails side of our pennies. Point to the words under the building. They read *one cent*. That means that a penny is worth one cent. If we had 2 pennies, we would have 2 cents. Can anyone tell me how many cents we would have if we had 3 pennies?
Child:	We would have 3 cents.
Teacher:	That's right. What if we had 7 pennies?
Child:	Seven cents.
Teacher:	Yes, we would have 7 cents if we had 7 pennies. Today we will begin the penny toss, an experiment, and collect data from it to put on our Graph. When we toss a coin, it will come up either heads or tails. Let's try it. What did it come up?
Child:	It came up heads.
Teacher:	Yes, this time the coin came up heads. Let's look at our Graph. The first strip has a picture of the heads side of a penny. Would anyone like to color the first space of the heads strip? Now let's toss the coin again.

Tell children that the penny toss is an experiment to learn about the chances of having a coin come up heads or tails. After the demonstration, ask children if they think the penny will come up all heads, all tails, or some of each. Tell them they can check their guesses by observing the Graph as it accumulates data throughout the month. Explain that each school day, one volunteer will toss a penny twice, and another volunteer will record the results on the Graph.

For Throughout the Month
Sample Dialogue

Teacher:	How many tosses have come up heads?
Class:	Ten tosses have come up heads.
Teacher:	Yes, and how many tosses have come up tails?
Class:	Twelve tosses have come up tails.
Teacher:	Do we have more heads or tails?
Class:	We have 2 more tails than heads.
Teacher:	How do you know?
Child:	It has 2 more colored squares than 10.
Teacher:	Yes, and can anyone tell us how many tosses we have made?
Child:	We tossed it 22 times.
Teacher:	Yes, we have tossed the coin 22 times. How did you figure this out?
Child:	I counted 10, 11, 12, 13, 14, 15, 16, 17, 18, 19, 20, 21, 22.
Teacher:	Let's all count the squares: 10, 11, 12, 13, 14, 15, 16, 17, 18, 19, 20, 21, 22.
Teacher:	This is a good way to count the total number of tosses. Do you think if we count by ones we will still get 22? Let's count and see. Do you think tails will be ahead at the end of the month? Why?

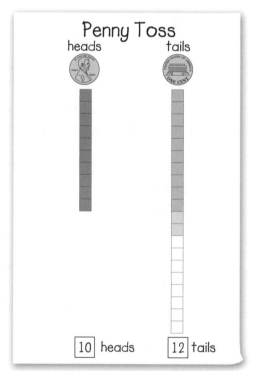

"Can anyone tell us how many tosses we have made?"

Child: Yes, it's ahead now and it's almost the middle of the month.

Teacher: Is there a chance that heads could be in the lead?

Child: Yes, the leader keeps changing.

Teacher: At the end of the month, let's see if your predictions match the results.

Discussions like this one should take place several times during the month to help children gain confidence in counting, comparing, and predicting.

To Sum Up

Probability Have children count and compare the numbers of heads and tails and determine if their predictions were correct. Talk about why the tosses for heads and tails may be getting nearer to half and half. Use the Graph to help children understand the monetary value of a penny by converting the number of heads and tails into pennies and then into cents.

Sample Dialogue

Teacher: Looking at our Penny Toss Graph, did we have more heads or tails?

Class: We had more heads.

Teacher: How many times did we get heads?

Child: We got it 21 times.

Teacher: Yes. Let's count them together—10, 20 (clap), 21. How many times did we get tails?

Child: We got it 19 times.

Teacher: That's right, the penny came up tails 19 times. When you made your predictions, who thought we would get more heads than tails? What did happen?

Child: Heads won because 21 is more.

Teacher: Did heads get a lot more?

Child: No, it won by only two.

Teacher: Were there more heads most of the month?

Child: No, sometimes tails won.

Teacher: So the number of heads and tails came out almost the same. Would anyone be willing to share why this happened?

Child: The penny has 2 sides.

Teacher: Yes. So it is just as likely to come up heads or tails way.

HELPFUL HINTS

- If you have a penny coin stamp or pictures of pennies, you might choose to use them to mark the spaces on the Graph.
- Coin toss experiments provide fun family math. You might ask that children work at home to tally the results of ten penny tosses. The children's tallies, which will vary greatly, can then be combined in class to create one very large graph. The larger sample will reflect results very close to half heads and half tails. Children can begin to see that the larger the sample, the more likely the results will reflect the true probability of heads and tails.

ESTIMATION AND MEASUREMENT

Concepts & Skills

- Estimate lengths
- Compare and order lengths
- Use the language of comparing
- Measure length using nonstandard units

Materials for February

A collection of common objects such as pencils, pens, pieces of yarn or string, paintbrushes, sticks, paper clips and so on; 31 connecting cubes of one color; paper for recording

Author Notes

"This month the children help to construct a connecting cube train by adding one cube each day. Children have an opportunity to observe the length of the train growing steadily over time, and are invited to guess how long it might be at the end of the month. Using this nonstandard unit to measure common objects, everyone has a chance to predict and discuss the outcome of comparing a classroom object with the length of the connecting cube train."

Ongoing Assessment

1. Can you find something that is just about as long as this train?
2. Show me how you know this train is longer than your shoe.
3. How many cubes long is this pencil?

Daily Routine

- Begin with just one connecting cube the first day. Identify objects that have about the same length.
- Each day add one more connecting cube to the first to create a connecting cube train. Record how many cubes long the day's train is.
- Have volunteers identify objects that might match the length of the train for the day and invite one volunteer to bring up an object or select an object from the classroom collection of items to compare.
- Before the object is matched to the connecting cube train, ask the children to predict whether the object will be too long, too short or just right.
- Model how to match one end of the object with the end of the connecting cube train. Have the class examine the match up and describe what they see, using words such as same, equals, longer, or shorter.

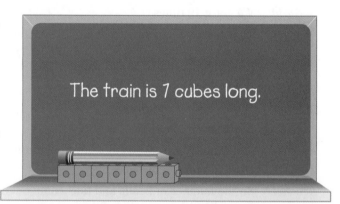

The train is 7 cubes long.

"The pencil and the train are the same length."

DISCUSSION

For Throughout the Month
Sample Dialogue

Teacher: Yesterday our train was 13 cubes long. How many cubes will our train be today?

Child: It will have 14 cubes.

Teacher:	That's right. Thirteen and one more is fourteen. Who thinks they can find something in the room that might be just about as long as our train today?
Child:	I think your pencil might be the same as the train.
Teacher:	Thank you for your suggestion. Let's hear what everyone else thinks. Put your hand up if you think the pencil has the same length as the train. Okay, and who thinks the pencil is shorter than the train? Longer than the train? Now who can tell me how we can find out the answer?
Child:	Put the pencil next to the train.
Teacher:	I will make sure the end of the pencil is right beside the end of the train. What do you see?
Child:	The pencil is shorter.
Child:	The train is longer.
Teacher:	Let's all count together to find out how many cubes long the pencil is.

Estimating, Comparing The following are questions which might be used to spark discussion of the day's results.

- Was today's comparison hard or easy for our class to predict?
- Do you see anything in our collection that is shorter than our connecting cube train? Longer? Show us.
- How many connecting cubes long do you think your pinky finger is? Your foot?
- How far do you think our connecting cube train will reach after we have added 4 more cubes? 10 more cubes?
- How far do you think our connecting cube train will reach by next week?

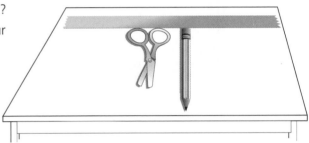

"The pencil is longer than the scissors."

For the End of the Month

Comparing, Counting Let the children use connecting cubes to measure objects in the classroom. You might want to set up an area for measuring. Place a long piece of tape on a table for children to use as a guide for matching the ends of the objects when they measure. Provide large paper clips linked together as an alternative nonstandard unit. After children have measured a few objects with both large paper clips and connecting cubes, encourage them to predict whether they will need more paper clips or more connecting cubes to equal the length of a new object.

HELPFUL HINTS

- *Guess and Match* Children can play this game alone or in pairs to practice estimating and comparing lengths. Players choose any two items. Guess if they are the same length or if one is longer. Match up the ends of the objects and find out.
- It is easy to extend the comparing activities to include the use of other nonstandard units. Craft sticks, dominoes, or tiles can all serve as nonstandard units of length. Children can place them end to end and count them to determine a measure.

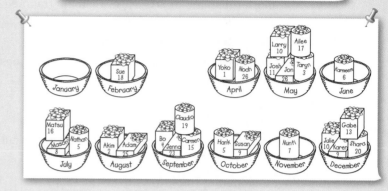

MARCH

Every Day Calendar

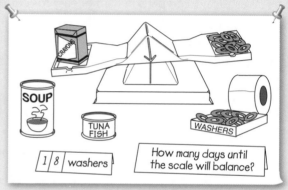

Birthday Baskets

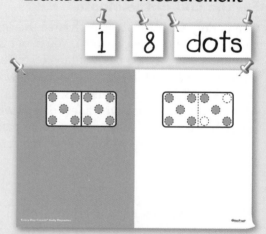

Estimation and Measurement

Nickel Toss

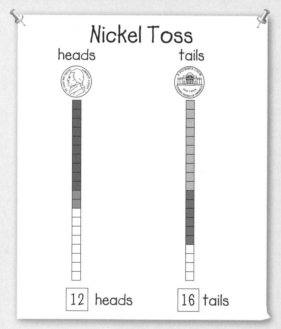

| 12 | heads |

| 16 | tails |

Graph

| 1 | 8 | dots |

Daily Depositor

Counting Tape

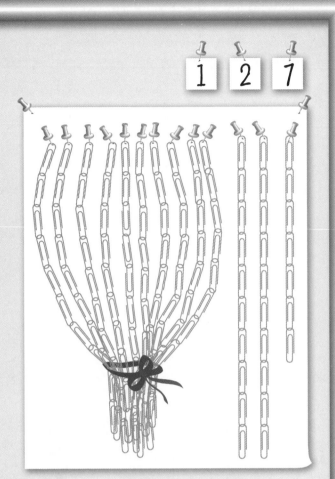

Clip Collection

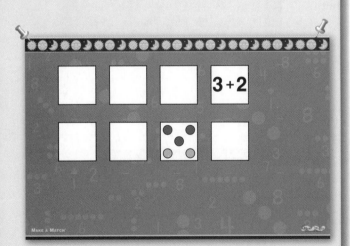

3 + 2

Domino Number Builder

MARCH ELEMENTS

use patterns to make predictions, use language of size comparison, recognize spheres

recognize and group quantities 1–31 by tens, fives, and ones

see 2 more, match combinations of small sets with combinations of numbers, practice spatial problem solving and use position words

count beyond 100, read 3-digit numbers, count and group by tens and ones, review counting patterns

recognize a nickel, conduct a probability experiment, build and use a bar graph

estimate weight, use language of comparing, use nonstandard units of weight

In March the Counting Tape and Clip Collection are used to familiarize children with quantities and numbers above 100. The Calendar shows a pattern with three sizes of spheres. The Depositor has children practice grouping by fives with double-fives dominoes. The Domino Number Builder invites children to match dot combinations with number combinations. Children explore chance by tossing nickels and creating the Graph from their findings. Estimation and Measurement introduces the use of nonstandard units of weight.

As children see relationships and make connections at different points in the year their moment of recognition should receive the same regard as did the observations of the first child who saw it. By showing joy at children's insights, you encourage even those with the least sophisticated number sense to get involved.

| Number & Operations | Algebra | Geometry | Measurement | Data & Probability |
| Problem Solving | Reasoning | Communication | Connections | Representation |

CALENDAR

Concepts & Skills

- Develop number sense
- Recognize, analyze, and extend patterns
- Use the language of comparison by size
- Recognize and describe spheres

Daily Routine

- Continue using Birthday Data as in previous months.
- Use the Calendar Pieces to initiate discussions using vocabulary of size comparisons.

Ongoing Assessment

1. Can you find a shape in the classroom that is like the shapes on the Calendar Pieces?
2. What size ball do you think we will see tomorrow?
3. Can you tell me two things that are changing in this Calendar pattern?

DISCUSSION

For the First Day

Comparing, Patterns, Algebraic Thinking Some balls are a solid color and some are striped, so a variety of patterns are available to explore this month. For the first time this year, three different-sized spheres appear on the Calendar. Use many different ways to describe the variation in sizes: *small, little, tiny; middle-sized, medium* or *in-between;* and *big* or *large.* You may also want to explore the language of *big, bigger, biggest.* A discussion similar to the following may help children with this language.

Sample Dialogue

Teacher: What do you notice about these three pieces for this month's pattern?

Child: They are different balls. They are different sizes.

Teacher: That's right. How could we describe the size of this first ball?

Child: It is little.

Teacher: Okay. What words could we use to describe the size of the second ball?

Child: It's in the middle.

Teacher: Oh, so could we call it the middle-sized ball?

Child: Yes.

Teacher: Now, what about the last ball or the third ball? How should we describe its size?

Child: It's big.

Teacher: Okay. We now have little, middle-sized and big balls Let's say that pattern.

Class: Little, middle-sized, big, little, middle-sized, big.

Teacher: Be thinking about some other ways that we could describe our size pattern. We will talk about this on another day.

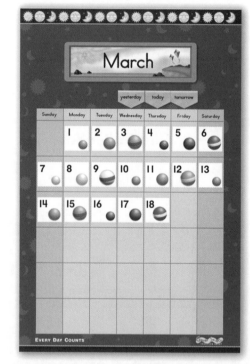

The March Calendar Pieces create an ABC pattern using small, medium-sized and large spheres (balls). The color of each new group of three balls is determined by the stripe of the previous ball.

For the End of the Second Week

Explain that a new pattern is beginning to appear on the March Calendar. Ask children to predict each day's color and size and to tell the date. Ideas to facilitate a discussion follow.

Algebraic Thinking To search for patterns and make generalizations:

- Talk to us about what you see on the March Calendar.
- Do you see anything besides the different sizes that keep repeating?
- In this pattern, do you think that the middle-sized ball will always come after the small ball?
- What do you notice about the solid balls and the striped balls?
- Does this keep happening over and over?
- What is the same about all of our large (big) balls?
- The colors of our balls keep changing. What do you notice about the colors?

Geometry To explore and describe spheres:

- In the world of Mathematics, we call this ball shape a sphere.
- Can you find any other sphere shapes in our classroom?
- How are spheres different from other shape?
- Can you find shapes that roll but are not spheres?

Let children use a variety of art materials or manipulatives to copy, extend, or create an ABC pattern of their own. Encourage them to build patterns using size, shape, position, texture and so on.

"The pattern is small, medium-sized, large, small, medium-sized, large."

"It goes big, bigger, biggest."

"The pattern is ABCABCABC."

"There is also a plain, plain, striped pattern. There are two patterns."

To Sum Up

On one of the last days in March, have children look closely at the Calendar and share with the class any patterns they see.

Identify the spaces on the Calendar that represent the last day of March and the first day of April. Explain that even though we are starting a new month, we know what day of the week the new month will begin with.

Number & Operations		Algebra	Geometry	Measurement		Data & Probability
Problem Solving		Reasoning	Communication		Connections	Representation

DAILY DEPOSITOR

Concepts & Skills

- Count with one-to-one correspondence
- Match quantities and numerals
- Read and write numerals to 31
- Group and count by fives and tens

Materials for March

4 Double Fives Dotted Dominoes (TR15), crayons

Ongoing Assessment

1. How many dots are on this domino?
2. Do we have more or less than 10?
3. How many more to get to 5? 10?

Author Notes

"Individual dots on the Double Fives Domino will be colored for this month's Daily Depositor. When a Domino of 10 dots is colored, it will be moved from the ones side of the Depositor to the tens side. Using yet another model for place value exploration gives children further opportunities to generalize this concept of collecting objects in the ones place and then grouping or moving them as ten to the tens place."

Daily Routine

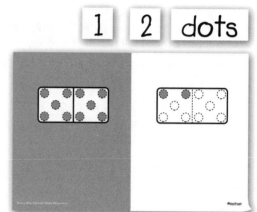

- Each day of March, color 1 dot on a Double Fives Domino. Display a *1* in the ones place on the Depositor.

- On Mondays fill in dots for Saturday and Sunday as well.

- When 10 dots have been colored, move the Domino to the tens side.

- From the 10th day on, have the class tell how many tens they see and how many extra ones.

- On the 11th day, put up a blank Domino on the ones side and continue the pattern of updating.

DISCUSSION

For Throughout the Month

On the first day of March, count with children the dashed circles on the Domino to verify that they will be collecting 10 dots on each card. Allow a volunteer to color in 1 dot on the Domino. Each day involve the children in talking about what they see. The following are examples of ideas that might encourage discussion throughout the month.

Counting, Place Value To encourage grouping, counting and instant recognition of small quantities:

- How many more to get to 5? 10?

- Do we have enough to make a group of ten?

- Do we have more or less than 10?

- Let's count the seven dots: 1, 2, 3, 4, 5, 6, 7. Now let's count on from 5. Five, 6, 7. Can we get to 7 by counting either way?

- (Point to the numeral in the ones place.) What does this tell us? (Point to the numeral in the tens place.) How about this number?

For the End of the Month

Take the Domino Cards off of the Depositor and focus on all of the different ways to count these dots. Count them by ones and by tens. Someone may even suggest counting by fives.

HELPFUL HINT

- The children may enjoy playing with a set of real dominoes. Have them spread out a set of dominoes from 1 to 5 and turn them over. Let them take turns flipping one domino over and saying how many dots are on the entire domino as fast as they can. Children continue playing until all the dominoes are turned over.

DOMINO NUMBER BUILDER

Concepts & Skills

- Visualize domino arrangements for 3 through 9
- Match quantities and numerals
- See sets from 3 to 9 as combinations of smaller sets
- Use spatial problem solving
- Understand and use positional words
- Understand "plus" sign

Materials for March

1–9 Dotted Domino Halves (TR9); 3–9 Number Combination Cards (TR17); Make a Match poster

Author Notes

"This month, the Daily Domino again becomes a Make a Match memory game, giving the children a chance to match quantities and number combinations (such as 3 + 2) using Dominoes and Number Cards. Children engage in spatial problem solving relying on visual memory to remember where each Domino and Number Card is in the arrangement of cards. Make a Match also helps children learn ordinal descriptions as well as other position language such as *top row*, *bottom row*, and *in the middle*, as you model the use of these words and they describe the location of the two cards they wish to turn over. Dominoes and Number Combination Cards 3 through 6 are explored until all matches are made and then Dominoes and Number Combination Cards for 7 through 9 are matched.

"The 5 Domino matches 3 + 2."

Ongoing Assessment

1. Did she turn over the first card or the second card?
2. Does this Domino match this Number Combination Card? Why not?
3. What Number Combination Card are you hoping to find?

Daily Routine

- The first day, randomly place the cards onto the poster face-down.
- A volunteer chooses two cards to turn over. If they are a match, both cards are removed. If they are not a match, they are returned face-down.
- Find one match per day until all matches for Dominoes and Number Combination Cards 3–6 and then 7–9 have been made.

DISCUSSION

For the Beginning of the Month
Sample Dialogue

Teacher: Today we are going to play Make a Match, our memory game with our Dominoes and the Number Combination Cards. Let's look at our cards. You will notice that some of our cards are dominoes and some show numbers and a special sign. Does anyone know what this sign (+) is between our numbers?   **MORE ▶**

Child: It means "plus".

Teacher: That's right. But what does "plus" mean?

Child: My brother does this.

Teacher: We have been reading our Number Combination Cards, 4 and 1. Well, this is a symbol that we can use instead of writing out the word "and" each time. It's a shortcut. We can still read our cards *3 and 2* even when we see this sign.

Teacher: Let's read these cards (1 and 2, 2 and 2, 3 and 2, 4 and 2, 5 and 2, 6 and 2, 7 and 2) Do you see a domino that matches one of these number cards?

For After Make a Match is Completed

Return cards face-up to the poster. Ask for volunteers to tell number stories about one of the cards, and let the class determine which card the story matches.

HELPFUL HINTS

- It is sometimes fun to give the children a supply of blank Dotted Dominoes for a number and let them see how many different ways they can color two reds and the rest blue.

- For a greater challenge place all the cards for 3–9 on the Make a Match poster at once.

Number & Operations	Algebra	Geometry	Measurement	Data & Probability
Problem Solving	Reasoning	Communication	Connections	Representation

COUNTING TAPE AND CLIP COLLECTION

Concepts & Skills

- Develop number sense
- Count and group by tens and ones
- Match quantities with numerals
- Compare and order quantities
- Count on and count back
- Discover number patterns and use mental math

Daily Routine

- Repeat the same sequence of colors used within each decade before 100 when putting up squares for the days after 100.

- Ask discussion questions that draw children's attention to the repeated pattern.

- Frequently count by tens and ones to help children become comfortable reading larger numbers.

Ongoing Assessment

1. What do you notice is the same about every red square?

2. Today is the 123rd day of school. Can you tell me what number will be on tomorrow's square?

3. Today we have 129 clips. How many clips will we have tomorrow?

DISCUSSION

For Throughout the Month

On the days of school after Day 100, children see the counting pattern 1 to 99 repeating on the Counting Tape. Help children observe the similarities between the numbers that are put on the Tape after Day 100 and the numbers that occurred earlier. If they discover the predictability of number sequences, they may develop confidence in counting larger quantities.

Patterns Frequent short discussions similar to the following example for Day 123 will help everyone focus on patterns.

Sample Dialogue

Teacher: What number will we write on today's square?

Class: We will write 123.

Teacher: Yes, today is the 123rd day of school. Can anyone tell me what number will be on tomorrow's square?

Child: Tomorrow will be 124 because today is 123.

Teacher: Yes, you used the counting pattern to decide what the next number would be. Let's look at the Counting Tape. Can anyone show me a similar group of numbers on the Tape?

Child: I see 22, 23, 24 way over there.

Teacher: Yes, we have seen this pattern before. Let's count from the first day after 100 to today. . . . Now let's count from Day 1 to Day 23. . . . Look at the colors of the squares with the numbers 22 and 23. They are yellow and red. Look at the squares with numbers 122 and 123. What do you see?

Child: I see yellow and red.

Teacher: Yes, the color of the squares with numbers 22 and 122 is yellow, and the color of the squares with numbers 23 and 123 is red. The numbers follow each other in a pattern just like the color of the squares follow a pattern on the Tape.

Counting, Place Value A discussion similar to the following for Day 130 will help children use the Clip Collection to focus on pattern, quantities, and groups.

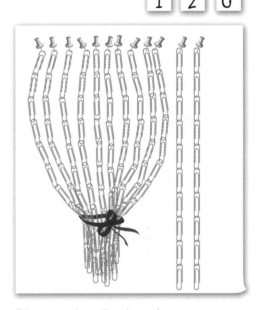

"How many clips will we have when we attach 1 more?"

Sample Dialogue

Teacher: Let's count by tens and ones to see how many clips we have in our collection.

Teacher & Class: 10, 20, 30, 40, 50, 60, 70, 80, 90, 100, 110, 120 (clap), 121, 122, 123, 124, 125, 126, 127, 128, 129.

Teacher: Yes, we have 129 clips—one chain of 100, two chains of 10, and 9 extra. Can anyone tell me how many clips we will have when we attach one for today?

Class: We will have 130.

Teacher: Yes, today we will have 130 clips. Will someone share with us how you figured this out?　　　　**MORE ▶**

Child: Well, 30 comes after 29.

Teacher: Yes, one more than 29 is 30, so one more than 129 is 130.

Since these discussions are taking you back to the first 23 days on the Tape, take some time to revisit some of the smaller numbers with the following questions.

Number Sense To develop number sense and the language of comparing:

- Which number is greater, 8 or 10?
- Which number is less, 12 or 7?
- What do we add to 6 to get to 7?
- Let's look at 3. How many squares do we need to get to 5?
- What would the neighbors for 10 be?
- What is the same about 12 and 22? What is different?

Patterns To encourage algebraic thinking by searching for patterns and making generalizations:

- What is the same about all of the red squares?
- Do you think that this will always be true for every red square?

Number & Operations   Algebra   Geometry   Measurement   Data & Probability
Problem Solving   Reasoning   Communication   Connections   Representation

GRAPH

Concepts & Skills

- Collect and record data from a probability experiment
- Analyze the results of a nickel toss to predict chances
- Count and compare quantities
- Recognize both sides of a nickel

Materials for March

Nickel Demonstration Coin cardstock, showing the heads and tails sides of the nickel; two sheets of Inch Squares Paper (TR14); crayons; a nickel

Author Notes

"The nickel toss provides an opportunity for children to become familiar with a nickel and identify it by color, size, weight, and whether it is showing heads or tails. Their observations should give you an opportunity to interject information about President Jefferson and have children recall facts about the penny discussed last month. In addition, children are exposed to the likelihood of getting heads or tails, and how to graph the results."

Setup

- Cut the Inch Squares Paper into strips of 10 squares.
- Arrange them in two long strips to create a 2-bar graph.
- Title the strips *heads* and *tails*.

Ongoing Assessment

1. How many times has our nickel come up heads so far?
2. How can we tell whether we have had more heads or more tails come up so far?
3. Why do you think both tosses came out about the same?

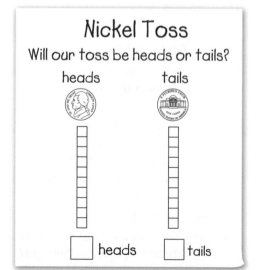

Daily Routine

- Each day assign two volunteers to the nickel toss. One partner tosses the coin twice as the other records each toss by coloring a space in the *heads* or *tails* strip.

- When a strip of ten is completed, put up another one. Shade each strip differently to help children count by tens and ones.

Discussion

For the First Day

Display the Demonstration Coin that shows both sides of the nickel and pass out a nickel to the class. Ask children to look at the picture and the coin in their hand and talk about what they see. Introduce the nickel, its monetary value, and the nickel toss in a discussion similar to the one that follows.

Sample Dialogue

"What do you notice about the nickel?"

Teacher: What do you notice about the nickel?

Child: It's silver.

Teacher: Yes, it is covered with nickel metal that gives it a silver-gray color. What coin did we learn about last month that was brownish-orange in color?

Class: That was the penny.

Teacher: Yes. Now, what else do you see on the nickel?

Child: One side has a face.

Child: One side has a building.

Teacher: Yes, a nickel has a face on one side and a building on the other. The face on the nickel is Thomas Jefferson. He was our third President and lived over 200 years ago during the same time period as George Washington, our first President. The building on the other side of the nickel is Jefferson's home in Monticello, Virginia. Remember that the penny had a face—President Lincoln's—on one side and a building—the Lincoln Memorial—on the other side. Just like the penny, some words are printed under the building on the nickel. The words on the nickel read *five cents*. Does someone remember the words on the penny?

Child: The penny reads *one cent*.

Teacher: That's right. Can someone tell me how many cents we would have if we had 5 pennies?

Class: We would have 5 cents.

Teacher: That's right. Let's look at our nickel again. It reads *five cents*. We just said that if we had 5 pennies, we would have 5 cents, too. If we have 1 nickel or if we have 5 pennies, we have the same number of cents. How many cents would we have if we had 1 nickel?

Child: We would have 5 cents.

More ▶

Teacher:	Yes! Today we will begin the nickel toss. We will toss it twice each day we are in school to see how many times it will come up heads and how many times it will come up tails. We will record the results on our Graph every day. Let's try it. What did it come up?
Child:	It came up tails.
Teacher:	Yes, this time it came up tails. Let's look at our Graph. The left side has a picture of the heads side of a nickel. The other side has a picture of the building, which we call the tails side of a nickel. Would anyone like to color the first space of the tails strip? Now let's toss the nickel again.

Collecting Data After the demonstration, ask the class if they think the nickel will come up heads all the time, tails all the time, or some of each. Tell them they can check their guesses by observing the graph as it accumulates data throughout the month. Explain that each day, one volunteer will toss a nickel twice and another volunteer will record the results on the graph. You also might want to keep a tally count of the heads and tails tossed in our coin toss. This will provide children with an opportunity to see data collected in a variety of ways. For the first five days, record the number of heads tossed and the number of tails tossed as well as the total tossed.

Discussion

For During the Month

Encourage children to count and compare by engaging them in a discussion similar to the Discussion on the penny toss (See pages 96–97.) Repeating these kinds of discussions will help children gain confidence in using these skills.

To Sum Up

Probability, Analyzing Data Have children count and compare the number of heads and tails and determine whether their predictions were correct.

Sample Dialogue

Teacher:	Look at our Nickel Toss Graph. Did we have more heads or more tails?
Class:	There were more tails.
Teacher:	How many times did we get tails?
Child:	We got tails 21 times.
Teacher:	Yes. Let's count them together: 10, 20 (clap), 21. How many times did we get heads?
Child:	We got heads 19 times.
Teacher:	That's right, the nickel came up heads 19 times. When you made your predictions, who thought we would get more tails than heads? What happened?

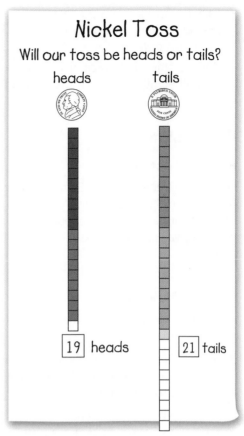

"Did we get more heads or tails?"

Child:	Tails won.
Teacher:	How do you know?
Child:	It has more squares.
Teacher:	Let's compare these numbers. If we partner them up, how many do not have a partner?
Child:	Two.
Teacher:	That's right, 2 do not have a partner. How many more heads would we need so they both had the same amount?
Child:	Two.
Teacher:	Were there a lot more tails or were they almost the same?
Child:	Almost the same.
Teacher:	Think back to last month's penny toss. Did it come out about the same for head and for tails?
Child:	Yes.
Teacher:	Why do you think both tosses come out about the same?

HELPFUL HINTS

- Some kindergartners may not be able to grasp the relationship between nickels and cents, but others may. It might be fun to explore counting the monetary value of 21 nickels. You might try grouping two nickels together and explaining that you have ten cents for each group of two nickels. Then have children join you in counting by tens as 10 cents, 20 cents, 30 cents, and so on.

- If you have a nickel coin stamp or pictures of nickels, you might want to use them to mark the spaces on the Graph rather than coloring them.

- Coin toss experiments provide fun family math. You might ask that children work at home to tally the results of ten nickel tosses. The children's tallies, which will vary greatly from one another, can then be combined in class to create one very large graph. The larger sample should be closer to half heads and half tails. Children can begin to see that the larger the sample, the more likely the results will reflect the true probability of heads and tails.

ESTIMATION AND MEASUREMENT

Concepts & Skills

- Match quantities and numerals
- Read and write numerals
- Group and count by tens
- Estimate and measure weight using nonstandard units

Materials for March

31 metal washers or other nonstandard units of weight; a balance scale, or a pair of teacher-made spring scales (see Helpful Hints); and a collection of small common objects to use in the scale

Author Notes

"This month the children will explore measurement by using a scale for collecting nonstandard units of weight. A common object such as a roll of masking tape or a box of crayons is placed on one side of the scale, and the units are placed on the other side, one unit per day. Early in the month the children guess the day on which they think the scale will balance. Every day the units are removed from the scale, then grouped into piles of ten, counted, and recorded. When enough units accumulate to balance the object, it is replaced with a heavier object for the class to consider.

This use of the scale is not intended to be a substitute for hands-on experience. Its purpose is to pique interest in weighing objects and using units to quantify various weights. When March passes, put the scale, units, and collection of common objects in a place where children can get to them. Children can pair up to estimate and weigh things on their own during selected times. Some may want to use their emerging number-writing skills to record their findings."

Daily Routine

- On the first day of March, introduce the balance scale. Have a volunteer place 1 washer on one side of the scale.
- Each day add 1 more washer and record the new total number of washers. On Mondays, add units for Saturday, Sunday, and Monday so the total is the same as the day's date.
- Around March 5, place a common object that weighs less than 31 washers (but more than 5 washers) on the other side of the scale.
- Let children suggest how many washers they think will be needed to balance the object. Record their guesses.
- Continue to add 1 washer a day. Occasionally allow the children to revise their estimates if they wish.
- When the scale balances, replace the object with a heavier one and repeat the estimation.

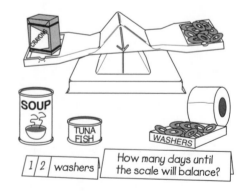

Ongoing Assessment

1. Do you think the scale might balance tomorrow? Why do you think so?
2. Do you think we will have to add a lot of washers or just a few to make the scale balance?
3. How many more washers do you think we will have to add to make the scale balance?

Discussion

For Throughout the Month

To count the washers each day, remove them all from the scale and group them into piles of ten and extras. Have the class tell you how many groups of ten and how many extra ones they see as you write down the tens and ones digits. A discussion similar to the following will help involve the children in the weighing process.

Sample Dialogue

Teacher: Today is March 12th, so how many washers will we have on the balance scale?

Class: There will be 12.

Teacher: Yes. How many piles of ten will I be able to make?

Child: One pile can be made.

Teacher: Let's see. Here are ten and 2 extras. Let's check to make sure they add up to 12. Count them with me. How shall I write this on the recording sheet?

Teacher & Class: One group of ten and 2, 12.

Teacher: Let's put the washers back on the scale and look at how close the scale is to balancing. Is the number of washers getting close to weighing the same as the box of crayons? On what day do you think the scale will balance and the two sides will weigh the same?

For further discussion opportunities, introduce the children to the activities described in the first two Helpful Hints below. Encourage children to explain their thinking as they make predictions.

Helpful Hints

- *What do you think? Which is heavier?* Ask a volunteer to help you model this partner activity using the scale and the common objects. One partner picks two objects, lifts them, passes them to the other partner to lift, then asks, "What do you think? Which is heavier?" The second partner makes a prediction followed by the other child agreeing or disagreeing. Then they each put one of the objects on the scale to find out for sure. The second partner gets to choose the two objects and asks, "What do you think?" on the next turn.

- *What do you think? How much does it weigh?* Model this activity using the scale, common objects, and washers or other nonstandard units. One person picks a common object, lifts it, passes it to the partner, and asks, "What do you think? How much does it weigh in washers?" Partners make their guesses and place the object on one side of the scale and place washers on the other side until the scale balances. Then they take the washers out and count them together. The second partner picks out the next object to be weighed and asks, "What do you think?"

- Review the rules for using the scale that were introduced in December Estimation and Measurement, page 71.

- To make a rubber-band spring scale see page 71.

APRIL

Every Day Calendar

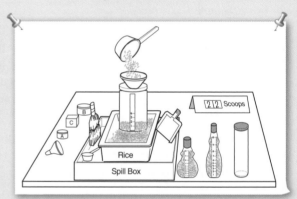

Birthday Baskets

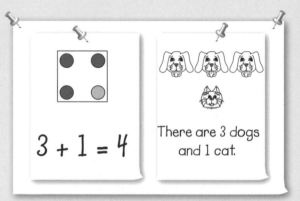

Estimation and Measurement

April Temperature Graph

warm
chilly, cool
very cold

Graph

$3 + 1 = 4$

There are 3 dogs and 1 cat.

Domino Number Builder

 | 128 | 129 | 130 | 131 | 132 | 133 | 134 | 135 | 136 | 137 | 138 | 139 | 140 | 141 | 142 | 143

 Counting Tape

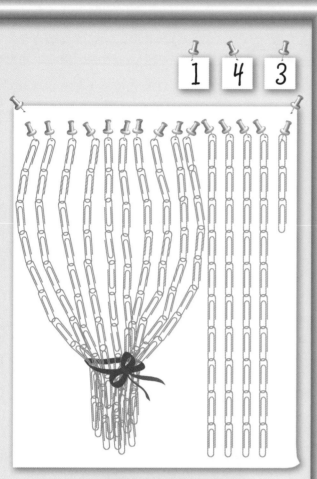

Clip Collection

Daily Depositor

APRIL ELEMENTS

In April, the Counting Tape and Clip Collection
continue with their progression of three-place
numbers. The Calendar and Birthday Data offer
more experiences with patterns and problem
solving. Once again the Graph associates outdoor
clothing with different levels of warmth to get a
glance at spring weather.

In some elements, new twists bring spring
freshness to Calendar Math. The Depositor uses
pennies and dimes equal to the day's date in cents
to expose children to these coins and their values.
The Domino Number Builder is used to introduce
writing number stories using words and symbols.
Estimation and Measurement exposes children to
measuring the capacity of various containers using
nonstandard units.

CALENDAR

Concepts & Skills
- Compare numbers
- Analyze and extend patterns
- Explore and describe spheres, cubes and cones
- Solve problems and use mental math

Materials for April
Cone-, cube-, and sphere-shaped objects (optional)

Daily Routine
- Use the 3-dimensional shapes on the Calendar Pieces to spark conversations about similar 3-dimensional shapes in the environment.
- Invite children to make predictions about the pattern and encourage them to share how they came up with their predictions so the group can see several approaches to a problem.
- Occasionally interpret the month's AABC pattern using body motions with three different body movements to create the pattern.
- Other times, have children use various art materials, collections, or manipulatives to copy, extend, or create their own versions of the AABC pattern.

DISCUSSION

For the First Day
Continue using Birthday Data in April as in previous months. Point out that April is the fourth month of the year. After volunteers have placed the April Present Pictures on the Calendar, ask children a few questions to get them thinking more. When questions have more than one correct response, acknowledge the one given and ask for additional responses. Variations of these questions can be asked throughout the month.

Counting, Comparing To encourage counting and comparing:
- Are there more birthdays this month or during your birthday month?
- Which month is the first month of the year? The tenth month?
- How many more months until your birthday month?
- How many birthdays come in April and March?
- Which month has fewer birthdays, February or April? How many fewer?

Ongoing Assessment
1. What shape is on April 2nd?
2. Which shape shows up in groups of 2?
3. What shape do you think will be on tomorrow's Calendar Piece?

The April Calendar Pieces create an AABC pattern using beach balls, baby blocks, and party hats.

For After the Second Week

Point out that a new pattern is appearing on the April Calendar. If possible, find 3-dimensional objects to compare to the pictures. Some ideas to facilitate discussions follow.

Three-dimensional Shapes To describe 3-dimensional shapes and find them in the environment, occasionally ask a question such as:

- We call the shape of a beach ball a sphere. Can anyone find any other spheres in the room?
- The baby block is a cube. A cube is a special kind of box shape. (Outline one face of the `cube` with your finger.) What shape do you see on this side? (Turn the cube and outline another face.) What shape do you see here?
- Does anyone see any cubes with square faces on all sides in the room? (There may not be any.)
- The party hat shape is a `cone`. Where have you ever seen other cones?

Take a shape walk through the school to find other examples of objects that resemble these 3-dimensional shapes.

Algebraic Thinking To search for patterns and make predictions:

- What shape did we put up on the 2nd day of April? The third day? The fifth day?
- What shape will appear in one day? In two days? In four days?
- What shape will appear next Tuesday? Next Friday?

These questions encourage a variety of counting on and mental math strategies. Some children will count all the spaces to the designated space. Others will use the pattern to help them.

Comparing, Fractions To foster an understanding of grouping, and fractions of a set:

- (on the 8th day) How many shapes do we have on the calendar so far? How many of them are the special box shape called a cube? (Oh, so 2 of the 8 shapes are cubes.)
- Do any of our shapes come in groups of two? Which shape? Let's count these groups of two.

To Sum Up

On one of the last days in April, ask children to share any patterns they see on the Calendar. The color pattern and shapes will make several diagonals stand out.

Before removing the Calendar pieces, focus on the last day of April and the first day of May. You may want to point out the day of the week that will be the first day of May, to be revisited tomorrow.

"There's 2 balls, then 1 block and 1 party hat, over and over."

"The beach balls make steps."

"There are always 2 balls."

DAILY DEPOSITOR

Concepts & Skills

- Recognize dimes and pennies
- Know the value of a dime and penny
- Count on from 10
- Read and write numerals to 30
- See combinations for 10

Materials for April

Dime Demonstration Coin cardstock, showing the heads and tails sides of the dime; 3 dimes and 10 pennies; two 3" × 6" clear pockets; Bank/Purse Background (TR18)

Author Notes

"This month the Daily Depositor collects a penny a day. The dime makes its first appearance this month when ten pennies can be exchanged for a dime on the tenth, the twentieth and the thirtieth. Children experience the fact that a single coin can have a value of several cents. Children more easily comprehend that the dime is worth ten cents when they witness the frequent exchanges. The Depositor boosts confidence by providing lots of practice counting up a very limited number of coins."

Daily Routine

- Beginning on the first of April, have a volunteer place one penny in the clear pocket on the ones side of the Depositor. Record a *1* in the ones place on the Depositor record.
- Continue adding a penny each day through the tenth. On this day, exchange the ten pennies for a dime. Place the dime in the pocket on the tens side of the Depositor as you explain what the dime is worth.
- Every day have the class check the total value of the coins by adding them together, using a variety of strategies. Then ask the children to tell you how to record this amount in tens and ones above the Depositor.

DISCUSSION

For the Tenth of the Month

Use the Dime Demonstration Coin to familiarize children with the appearance of the dime. This is a good time to pass out real dimes to the class. Ask children to look at the dimes in their hands and to find some things that make the dime different from the penny. They may mention that the dime is smaller and doesn't have a building on the back. To conclude the discussion, you may want to ask children to describe some of the things they notice are similar about the dime and penny.

Ongoing Assessment

1. What coins do you see in the Depositor today?
2. Do we have enough pennies to make a trade?
3. How many more pennies do we need to make a trade?

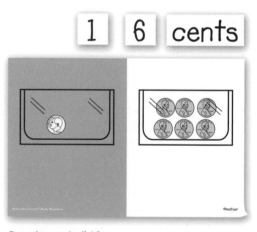

Depositor on April 16.

Sample Discussion

Teacher: What coins do we see in the Depositor today?

Child: I see 1 dime and 6 pennies.

Teacher: Let's count to see how much these coins are worth all together. We can start at 10, since the dime is worth 10 cents. Let's count on. Ten, 11, 12, 13, 14, 15, 16.

Class: They are worth 16 cents.

Teacher: So we started with the coin worth the most, the dime, and then we counted the pennies. Let me record that. I'll write a *1* for the dime on the tens side and a *6* for the total of 6 cents on the ones side. Let's read it together.

Teacher & Class: 1 group of ten and 6 is 16 cents.

Teacher: What is the same about these coins? How are they different? Which coin is larger? Which coin is worth the most? Would you rather have a penny or a dime? Why?

For the End of the Month

At the end of April, remove the coins from the Depositor and place them in a resealable plastic bag. Place a set of matching coins in another bag and make the two sets of coins available for the activities described in Helpful Hints.

HELPFUL HINTS

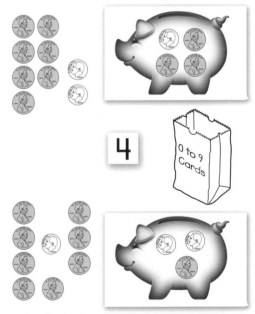

Coin Collecting Game

- *Coin Collecting:* Gather the class into a circle on the floor so everyone can see you and a volunteer play the game. You should each have a Bank/Purse Background (TR18) for your "bank" and a bag of coins (3 dimes and 10 pennies) to spill out on the floor. Take turns drawing (and putting back) a 0–9 Card (TR3) from a sack and placing this number of pennies in your bank. Imitating the Depositor whenever ten pennies accumulate in your bank, trade for a dime. The first person to accumulate 30 cents or more is the winner. A variation of this game would be to accumulate pennies only.

- *Going Shopping:* Label a few trinkets or pictures of store items with pretend prices ranging from 5 cents to 20 cents. Demonstrate with a partner how to take turns playing the roles of the customer and the clerk. The customer gets to choose something to buy and tries to get out coins that add up to the price. The clerk shares his or her way of counting up the coins to check the payment.

- There is no adequate substitute for using real coins with young children. Telling the class you trust them to take care of the coins so they can be used over and over during the year helps to build confidence.

- Let children know that the dime depicts President Franklin Roosevelt, who served over 50 years ago. The picture on the back is the torch of liberty between sprigs of laurel and oak.

DOMINO NUMBER BUILDER

Concepts & Skills

- Visualize domino arrangements for 2 through 9
- See sets 2 to 9 as combinations of smaller sets
- Tell addition stories
- Use words and symbols to record addition stories

Materials for April

Completed Domino Records from October, December, and February; construction paper, preferably 12" × 18"

Author Notes

"This month children will use the two-colored Domino Records to tell addition stories and record them using the plus sign in number sentences."

Daily Routine

- Beginning with the quantity 2, each day display the three different Domino records for that day's quantity. For the quantity 2, show one with all dots blue, one with 1 red dot, and one with 2 red dots.
- Have the class identify the number of reds, the number of blues, and the number in all.
- Invite a volunteer to tell a story that corresponds with one of the cards displayed for that day.
- Periodically record the story in words and help the class to write a number sentence to accompany it. Record the stories on separate sheets of paper and put them together to make a class Number Story Book.

Ongoing Assessment

1. Quick as you can, how many dots are on this Domino?

2. Can you tell me a number story to go with this Domino?

3. Can you tell me a number sentence for this Domino?

DISCUSSION

For the Beginning of the Month

Discuss the idea that each Domino shows a different way to make the total. Encourage students to use instant recognition instead of counting the dots whenever possible.

Sample Dialogue

Teacher: Let's look at our Dominoes. How many dots are colored on this Domino?

Child: There are 5 blue dots.

Teacher: How about this one?

Child: There are 3 blue dots and 2 red dots.

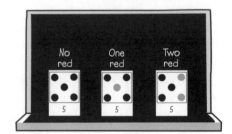

"Can you tell me a story about one of these Dominoes?"

Teacher: Is this another way to make 5? Let's count and make sure. We can count on. Three, 4, 5. We have 5 in all. How about our last Domino?

Child: It's 4 blue and 1 red and that makes 5, too.

Teacher: Who wants to share a story about 5 using one of our Dominoes?

Child: I have 3 goldfish and 2 guppies. That means I have 5 fish.

Teacher: We can write this in words using letters or we can write a number sentence using numbers. To show "three and two are five" we write *3 + 2 = 5*. I am going to write your story using words and numbers on this paper and put a small copy of your picture at the top of the page. Will you please draw a picture to go with your story? We will keep all of these pages to make a book.

If the children have difficulty choosing among three choices for their story, ask for a story to match one specific domino.

"I have 3 goldfish and 2 guppies."

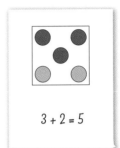
3 + 2 = 5

COUNTING TAPE AND CLIP COLLECTION

Concepts and Skills

- Count and group by tens and ones
- Match quantities with numerals
- Compare and order quantities
- Count on and count back
- Discover number patterns and use mental math

Daily Routine

- This month begin to have children estimate how long the tape will be when Day 180 appears.
- Frequently count by tens and ones to help children begin to understand place value in 3-digit numbers.

Ongoing Assessment

1. How many clips do we have today?
2. How many clips would be left if we took off this group of 100?
3. Can you tell me about a pattern you see on the Counting Tape?

133 134 135 136 137 138 139 140 141 142 143 144 145 146

DISCUSSION

For Throughout the Month

Revisit the patterns on the Counting Tape, discussing why they are patterns, and encouraging the children to make generalizations about these patterns. See March, page 107, for a sample dialogue to help children see the relationship between numbers less than 100 and the corresponding numbers greater than 100. See October, page 40, for examples of the kinds of questions to be adapted for larger numbers. Continue to focus on the numbers for yesterday, today, and tomorrow, or number neighbors.

"This is a pattern because it repeats."

"We keep seeing the blue square right after the green square."

"We know that every pink square will have a 3 on it."

"I see numbers repeating in the same order."

While most kindergartners may not be ready to focus on challenging questions about groups of tens, some will be ready for this enrichment. Ask questions that emphasize the similarities between the numbers before and after 100 and focus on groups of tens. For example:

• Today is Day 146. What day was it 10 days ago? 20 days ago? 30 days ago?

• If today were Day 46, what day would it have been 10 days ago? 20 days ago? 30 days ago?

Have children share how they figured out their answers. Point out the similarities between their answers for days before and after Day 100.

HELPFUL HINT

• Encourage children to guess how far the Counting Tape might reach if school were to last until Day 200.

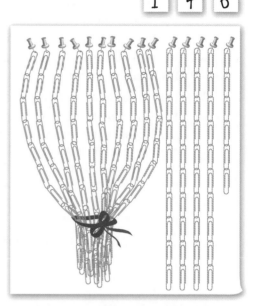

"How many clips do we have today?"

Number & Operations	Algebra	Geometry		Measurement	Data & Probability
Problem Solving	Reasoning		Communication	Connections	Representation

GRAPH

Concepts & Skills

• Collect and record data on a graph
• Reading and interpret data on a picture or bar graph
• Count and compare quantities
• Understand temperature

Materials for April

Every Day Graph (TR8), Clothing Markers (TR13), completed Graphs from November and January

Author Notes

"The Graph provides a record of clothing appropriate for temperatures in April. Graphing clothing again this month, as in November and January, allows the class to compare the fall and winter temperatures in your area with the temperatures that are occurring in spring."

Setup

• With the old November and January Graphs in view, allow children to tell you how to construct the April Graph so that it will be easy to compare the information gathered during the three different seasons.

Daily Routine

• Each day have the class talk about the temperature outside and how it is reflected in what they would wear outside.

Our April Temperature Graph

warm | chilly, cool | very cold

- Have a volunteer attach the appropriate Clothing Marker to the Graph.
- Occasionally invite children to predict how the completed April graph will compare to the January and November Graphs.

DISCUSSION

For Throughout the Month

Point to the November and January Graphs and ask children to indicate by a show of hands who thinks there will be more warm days in April than in the fall or winter. How about chilly days—fewer or the same? Warm days? Cold days? It will be interesting to see how the three temperature samples compare by the end of the month.

Refer to January's Discussion for other sample questions (page 81).

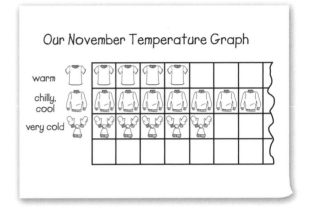

For the End of the Month

Analyze Data Focus children's attention on the three Graphs showing fall, winter, and spring temperatures as reflected by pictures of different clothing. Before making any comparisons, count up the total number of days represented on each Graph to make sure the samples are close enough in size to make a fair comparison. Each Graph should have 15 to 20 temperature markers. You might start with open-ended questions such as:

- What do we know about our fall, winter, and spring temperatures from what we see on these Graphs?

- What do these Graphs tell us?

After children have offered many observations and comparisons of their own, you might follow up with a few of these more specific questions.

- Which season had the greatest number of hot days? The greatest number of warm days?

- Which season had nearly the same number of warm days as cool days?

- Which seasons have nearly the same number of cool days?

- Which were the best months for riding a bike?

- Which month had the greatest number of days with your favorite temperature?

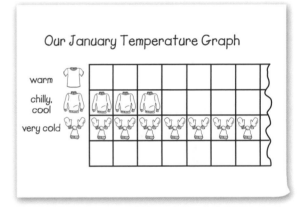

HELPFUL HINTS

- If your school year includes a vacation break in April, you will need to keep a record of the temperatures during vacation and update the Graph when everyone returns. Otherwise, the April sample at month's end will be too small to compare to the November and January data.

- Have children use the same means of marking the Graph that was used in November and January to make it easy to compare the Graphs from the three seasons.

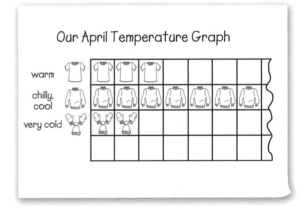

ESTIMATION AND MEASUREMENT

Concepts & Skills

- Counting with one-to-one correspondence
- Matching quantities and numerals
- Reading and writing numerals to 30
- Grouping and counting by tens
- Measuring capacity using nonstandard units

Materials

Dishpan of rice placed in a large shallow box; funnel; whisk broom; dustpan; 4 clear containers in various shapes and similar in capacity (minimum $2\frac{1}{2}$ cups); an assortment of other clear plastic containers with a variety of shapes and capacities; a measuring scoop ($\frac{1}{4}$ cup) labeled One Scoop, 0–9 Digit Cards (TR3) for recording the day's total

Ongoing Assessment

1. How many scoops of rice have we collected so far?

2. How high do you think the rice will be when we have poured in 10 scoops?

3. Look at the two containers that are each holding ten scoops. Why do you think the rice comes up higher on one of them?

Author Notes

"This month capacity is explored by adding one scoop of rice to a container and marking the new level each day. Whenever ten scoops accumulate in a container, a new empty container is introduced to receive the next scoop. The total number of scoops is recorded and read each day. This measurement experience gives children a chance to estimate and measure capacity. One intent is to encourage children's natural interest in exploring volume. The idea that units of capacity remain constant when they take up space in different-shaped containers is quite a sophisticated concept. Children enjoy experimenting and finding out how much different containers will hold."

"Today we have 24 scoops."

Daily Routine

- Each day, have a volunteer pour one scoop of rice into the first container and mark the level of the rice on the outside. Record a *1* in the ones place on the recording sheet.

- Continue adding and marking one scoop each day until the tenth of the month. Record the total. On Mondays, add a scoop for Saturday, Sunday, and Monday so the total is always equal to the day's date.

- On the 11th, place a new empty container beside the first container and pour the 11th scoop into it.

- From now on, have the class tell you how many containers of ten scoops and how many extra scoops have accumulated as you record the total. Continue this pattern of updating, bringing out a new container after every ten scoops.

For Throughout the Month

Introduce the rice setup on the first of April. As often as possible, involve children in talking about what they see as they look at the containers. The following are examples of questions that might encourage discussion throughout the month.

Comparing, Estimating To encourage the language of comparing and making predictions:

- How many scoops of rice have we collected so far?

- Why do you think the marks that show the scoops in the different containers are sometimes close together and sometimes far apart?

- Look at the two containers that are each holding ten scoops. Why do you think the rice comes up higher on one of them?

- Do you think the amount of rice in the two containers is the same or do you think there is more rice in one of them? Why?

- How can we find out if the amount of rice is actually the same?

HELPFUL HINTS

- When March comes to an end, make the rice setup, the calibrated containers, the scoop, and several unbreakable containers available to children to explore with a partner during "choosing times" in the weeks ahead. The activities described here encourage lots of firsthand experience comparing and measuring.

- *What do you think? How many scoops will it hold?* Ask a volunteer to help you model this partner activity. Choose one of the containers labeled A, B, C, D, and so on, and ask your partner, "What do you think? How many scoops will it hold?" You and your partner look at the scoop and the container and make guesses. Then your partner holds the funnel in place as you count the scoops of rice it takes to fill the container. Did you guess too many scoops, too few, or just about the right number? Let your partner choose the next container and ask you, "What do you think?"

- Another version of the same activity is to fill a container with rice and pour it into one of the empty containers that was calibrated during the month. Children read the scoop markings on the calibrated container to determine the number of scoops. Children enjoy testing their findings by measuring again, using a different calibrated container to see if the number of scoops comes out the same.

- Since the capacity of most of the containers will include a fraction of a scoop, some teachers fill the containers to the level of the last possible full scoop and draw a line across. These lines tell the children when to stop scooping.

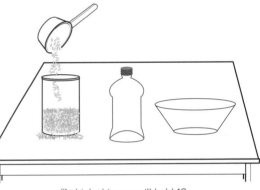

"I think this one will hold 12 scoops. What do you think?"

MAY

Every Day Calendar

Birthday Baskets

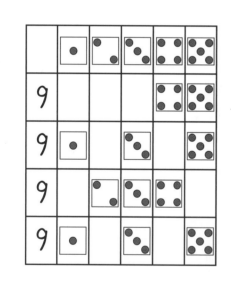

Domino Number Builder

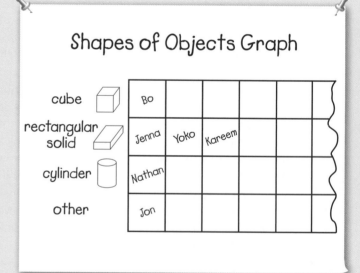

Shapes of Objects Graph

cube	Bo					
rectangular solid	Jenna	Yoko	Kareem			
cylinder	Nathan					
other	Jon					

Graph

150 151 152 153 154 155 156 157 158 159 160 161 162 163 164 165

 Counting Tape

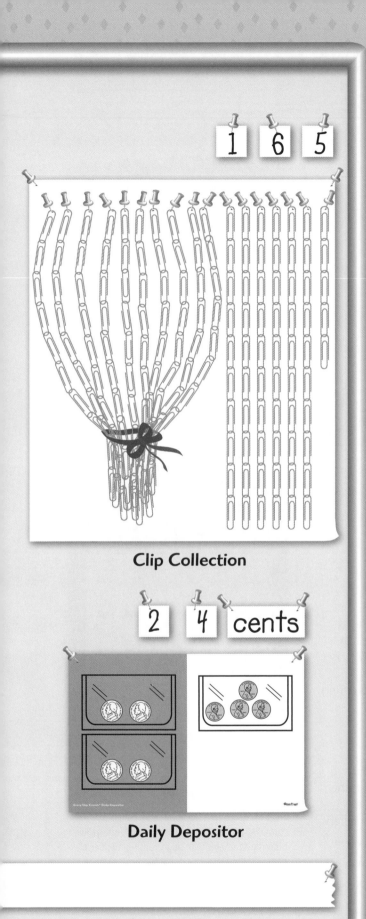

Clip Collection

Daily Depositor

Calendar Math offers meaningful math activities right up to the last day of school. The Graph focuses on different kinds of solids through a container collection. The Daily Domino uses problem solving to explore quantities to 9. If your school year extends into June, continue with the Calendar Math elements you wish. If you want to cut back, end with the elements we began with in September—the Counting Tape and Clip Collection, Calendar, and Birthday Data.

As the year comes to a close, you may want to question children about what they remember and have enjoyed most in Calendar Math. Graphing everyone's responses to the question, "Which part of Calendar Math helped me learn the most?" might provide a fitting end-of-the-year activity. While no two groups are alike, children's answers might help you to evaluate your successes and plan for modifications next year.

Number & Operations	Algebra	Geometry	Measurement	Data & Probability
Problem Solving	Reasoning	Communication	Connections	Representation

CALENDAR

Concepts & Skills

- Know the days of the week in order
- Know the names of the months
- Read, compare, and order numbers 1 to 31
- Analyze and extend patterns
- Compare numbers
- Explore a growing pattern

Daily Routine

For May

- Explain that this month's pattern is a different kind of pattern and it will not show up right away.
- As you add one new Calendar Piece each day, allow volunteers to guess what color the butterfly might be, and explain their thinking.
- Continue to use Yesterday, Today, and Tomorrow Markers, and discuss Birthday Basket data as in past months.

For June

- Look again at the pattern used in May, or if children are ready for a greater challenge, focus discussion on the number of wings.

DISCUSSION

For the Beginning of May

Tell children that this month's pattern is different from other patterns and it won't show up right away. In the beginning of the month just continue using Birthday Data as in prior months. Point out that May is the fifth month of the year. After volunteers have placed the May Present Pictures on the Calendar, ask questions that encourage ordering, counting, comparing, and problem solving.

For After the Second Week in May

It is possible that this may be the first time that your children will have seen a growing pattern. Let them simply make observations about this month's pattern with the butterflies on the calendar. Asking these questions will facilitate a discussion and might even help some children discover the pattern.

Algebraic Thinking To recognize and explore a pattern that grows:

- Would someone like to point to each butterfly and say its color out loud?
- Let's say the colors of the butterflies again and clap every time we come to an orange piece.
- Does anybody notice anything about how many times we clapped?

Ongoing Assessment

1. What color butterfly was on yesterday's date?
2. How many orange butterflies do you think there will be in this group?
3. What will the date be the next time we see a yellow butterfly?

The May and June Calendar Pieces create a ABABBABBB growing pattern in which one yellow butterfly alternates with an increasing number of orange butterflies.

- How many orange butterflies do you see in this group?
- Is there one orange butterfly that is all alone? Do you see a group of two butterflies?
- What do you notice about the orange butterflies? (Children will see that we keep adding more. There are many more orange butterflies than yellow butterflies. Someone usually notices that there is 1 orange butterfly, then 2 orange butterflies, followed by 3 orange butterflies).
- You know that a pattern is something that happens over and over again. What keeps happening over and over with the number of orange butterflies? (The number of orange butterflies goes up by one, over and over, like counting.)

If children seem to recognize a pattern, explain that this is called a growing pattern, since it grows by one over and over again. Continue to revisit this idea of a pattern that grows throughout the month. You many still have some children who are unsure of this new thinking. It will be revisited next month and again in first grade.

For the Month of June

You may again choose to look again at the butterfly pattern of May. Or if the children are ready for an even greater challenge, you may want to focus on the number of wings in each set of orange butterflies, which repeatedly increase by twos.

Also be sure to also point out that June is the sixth month of the year, and to complete the Birthday Data with June birthdays, as always.

HELPFUL HINTS

- If any summer birthdays have not been recognized as "unbirthdays," it might be fun to set aside a special time to celebrate so that no child will feel overlooked.
- Help children make their own summer wall calendars to take home. Staple together a cover sheet and three Calendar Records (TR2) for June, July, and August. Have children draw pictures on the backs of the first three pages and write a 1 in the correct space of each month. Then children can fill in with numbers and a pattern for each month as the summer unfolds. You'll want to encourage parents to put the Calendar up where they will be reminded to use it to talk with their child about upcoming events, as well as the numbers and patterns appearing each month.

DAILY DEPOSITOR

Concepts & Skills

- Recognizing dimes, nickels, and pennies
- Knowing the value of a dime, nickel, and penny
- Counting on from 5
- Reading and writing numerals to 30
- Seeing combinations for 5

Materials for May

Nickel Demonstration Coin cardstock; 6 nickels and 5 pennies; four
3" × 6" clear pockets

Author Notes

"This month the Daily Depositor collects a penny a day. Whenever five
pennies accumulate, they are traded for a nickel. Children again
experience the fact that a single coin can have a value of several cents.
Children more easily comprehend that the nickel is worth five cents
when they witness the frequent exchanges. The Depositor boosts
confidence by providing lots of practice counting up a very limited
number of coins. Be sure to give the children the opportunity to explore
the physical characteristic of the nickel early on in the month. Ask
children to describe some of the things they notice are similar about the
nickel and penny."

Daily Routine

- Each day have a volunteer place one penny in the clear pocket on the
  ones side of the Depositor. On Mondays, add a penny for Saturday,
  Sunday, and Monday.
- Record the total on the Depositor record.
- On the fifth day, exchange the five pennies for a nickel as you explain
  that a nickel is worth five cents.
- On the tenth day, exchange the second 5 pennies for a nickel and
  place the 2 nickels in the tens place.
- Whenever another 2 nickels have accumulated, move them to a new
  pocket on the tens side.

DISCUSSION

For the Tenth of the Month

On the sixth through the tenth, as you continue to add a penny a day,
practice counting the nickel as five cents to get the day's total. On the
tenth day, when the two nickels are moved to the tens place, revisit the
value of the nickels and the variety of ways to make ten with coins.
Every day have the class check the total value of the coins by adding
them together using a variety of strategies including counting by fives
or tens.

Ongoing Assessment

1. Can we make a trade today?
2. How much do we have in the Depositor today?
3. How many more days until we can make a trade?

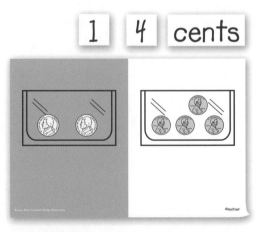

"Will we be able to trade for a nickel tomorrow?"

For the End of the Month

At the end of May, you may want to use your large demo coins to represent various amounts of money. Draw a digit card out of a bag and ask a volunteer to show this amount with the large coins. You may choose to work with pennies, nickels, or dimes or any combination of these coins depending on the experience level of your children.

Number & Operations		Algebra	Geometry	Measurement		Data & Probability	
Problem Solving		Reasoning	Communication		Connections		Representation

DOMINO NUMBER BUILDER

Concepts & Skills

- Use the 1 to 5 dominoes to make the quantities 1–9
- Count on
- Match quantities and numerals
- See sets 1–9 as combinations of smaller sets

Materials for May

Completed blue Domino Records for the quantities 1 to 5, Domino Total Record Sheet (TR19)

Author Notes

"This month children will search for all the different ways to build numbers 1 to 9 using the 1 to 5 dominoes. This provides children with concrete problem-solving experience building quantities using smaller sets."

Daily Routine

- Display all of the Dominoes for 1 to 5 that have been colored in blue.
- On 9 days of the month, focus on one of the numbers 1–9. Ask children to think about the day's number and decide how they can make that quantity by combining the Dominoes.
- Record their solutions on the Domino Totals Records by copying the Dominoes being added.

DISCUSSION

For Nine Different Days
Sample Dialogue

Teacher: Looking at our Dominoes, can you tell me one way we can make 5 using one or more of these Dominoes?

Child: We could use just the 5 Domino.

Teacher: Great! That is one way. Does anyone else have another way to make 5?

Child: We could use the 4 and the 1 Dominoes.

Teacher: Four and 1 more equals 5. Any others?

Child: I think that 3 and 2 will work.

MORE ▶

> ### Ongoing Assessment
>
> 1. Can we use these 2 Dominoes to make 5?
> 2. Can you find one way to make 6 from these Dominoes?
> 3. Tell me all the ways you can make six from these Dominoes.

Domino combinations for 5

Teacher: Well, let's try that and see if it works (pointing to the 3 Domino). If we start with the larger Domino—the three—and count on, then it will help us to figure this out. Any other solutions? (pause) OK, then let's draw the Dominoes in our chart to show the different combinations we have found.

Discussions like this provide children with experiences in counting on and seeing several different combinations for the same numbers. Continue to search for solutions up through the number 9.

HELPFUL HINT

- After 9 days, or in June, if the children have enjoyed this activity, you may want to put up two sets of 1 to 5 Dominoes and try the same activity over again. Examples of the variety of solutions possible for the fourth day using two sets of 1 to 5 Dominoes might be 1 four, 2 twos, 2 ones and 1 two, and 1 three and 1 one.

Number & Operations	Algebra	Geometry	Measurement	Data & Probability
Problem Solving	Reasoning	Communication	Connections	Representation

COUNTING TAPE AND CLIP COLLECTION

Concepts & Skills

- Develop number sense
- Count with one-to-one correspondence
- Count and group by tens and ones
- Match quantities with numerals
- Compare and order quantities
- Count on and count back
- Discover number patterns and use mental math

Ongoing Assessment

1. What color square do you think we will put up today?

2. How many more squares will we put up before we use another one the same color as today?

3. How many clips will we have when we put up the next blue square?

Daily Routine

- Frequently look back at the whole Tape during discussions.
- Toward the very end of the year involve children in wrap-up activities described in Helpful Hints.

DISCUSSION

For Throughout the Month

Pattern Encourage children to share observations about the way the counting pattern for numbers greater than 100 is like the pattern for numbers less than 100.

Number Sense To help children develop number sense, continue to include questions that promote counting on, counting back, and comparing. Use the Clip Collection to help children match numbers with quantities and practice grouping by tens.

HELPFUL HINTS

- On one of the last days of school, ask children how far the clips in the Clip Collection might reach if they were all connected. After listing their ideas connect all the clips so they can check their guesses.

- Take down the Counting Tape and reconstruct it. Cut the Tape into ten-number intervals, handing out strips 1–10, 11–20, 21–30, and so on, to individual children. Ask children to count the numbers on the first section of the Tape. Then have them point to the child they think should bring up the next strip of ten numbers, and then the next child, until all the strips have been put back in order.

- Construct a giant hundred chart. Children pin up the decade strips of the Counting Tape in order, one below the other, ending in 91–100. Have children begin another giant hundred chart beside the first, beginning with 101–110. Ask children to point out similarities and differences between the two charts. What do they notice? What do they see? Both charts provide a focus for pattern searches which help children see the predictability of the counting sequence.

- Children can color Blank Hundred Charts (TR20) to match the large one formed with the cut-apart Counting Tape. Then copies can be made and children can take them home in June to mark off the days of summer vacation. Ask, "Do you think you will have marked off 100 days before you return to school at the end of summer?"

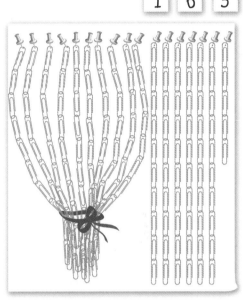

1 6 5

"How many clips would be left if we took off the group of 100?"

Number & Operations	Algebra	Geometry	Measurement	Data & Probability
Problem Solving	Reasoning	Communication	Connections	Representation

GRAPH

Concepts & Skills

- Read and interpret data on a picture or bar graph
- Count and compare quantities
- Recognize three-dimensional shapes in the environment
- Describe cylinders, rectangular solids, and cubes
- Name and identify circles, rectangles and squares

Materials for May

A collection of containers brought in by children from home and labeled A, B, C, D, and so on; copies of a parent letter for class members (see Helpful Hints); Every Day Graph (TR8); watercolor pen; 3 blank big books or large posters; permanent marker.

Ongoing Assessment

1. What shape do we have the most of now?

2. How many containers have been brought in so far?

3. What do we know about our collection of containers by looking at our Graph today?

© Great Source. Copying is prohibited.

Author Notes

"This month children work with three-dimensional shapes that have been discussed throughout the year: cylinders, rectangular solids, and cubes. The children will look for examples of these shapes in the environment and bring in a container or other discarded object from home that fits into one of these shape categories. The growth of the class collection will be recorded on a graph. Emphasis will be placed on helping children correctly use geometric terms to describe the shapes and distinguish characteristics that make each group of shapes unique."

Shapes of Objects Graph

	cube	Bo					
	rectangular solid	Jenna	Yoko	Kareem		
	cylinder	Nathan				
	other	Jon				

Setup

- During the first week, engage the children in helping create a display of the three shapes.

Daily Routine

- The first week introduce one 3-D shape each day. Show the class two or three examples of that shape and have children describe how they are alike.

- Each day thereafter, ask children who have brought containers to show them to the class.

- Have the group classify each container as a "can shape" or cylinder, a "rectangular box" or rectangular solid, a "square box" or cube, or other. Ask children to explain their classifications.

- Then have the day's contributors mark the Graph so all the containers brought in that day are recorded.

- Once or twice a week, ask the class to suggest a few facts revealed by the Graph. The collection can be kept on a small desk or table near the bulletin board.

DISCUSSION

For the Beginning of the Month

Geometry Display a poster with pictures of examples of the three shapes the class will be discussing, such as a teacher's mug, a sugar cube, and a book. Add your observations, if needed, so the critical attributes will be pointed out.

For cylinders (cans, spice jars, cardboard tubes, and so on):
  They are round and they roll.
  The faces or the openings on the two ends are matching circles.
  They will stand on their faces.

For rectangular boxes (shoe box, brick, chalkboard eraser, paperclip box, woodblock, and so on):
  They have six flat faces.
  The faces are in the shape of rectangles.
  They stack easily and do not roll.

For cubes (sugar cube, photo cube, wooden cube, and so on):
  They are all rectangular boxes.
  Their faces are all special rectangles called squares.

For the First Week

Three-dimensional Shapes, Sorting Search for other examples of three-dimensional shapes in the classroom. Label a poster or a big book with the name and a sketch of the day's shape. Invite children to cut out pictures of common objects that represent the shape from advertising supplements of magazines. These pictures of real-world three-dimensional geometric shapes can then be pasted onto the poster or pages of the big book.

For the Second Week

Collect Data Have children look for one or two discarded unbreakable items at home that can be added to the class collection of cylinders, rectangular solids, cubes, and other items. The item must be one the family no longer needs. See sample letter in Helpful Hints. With the children's help, assemble a Graph that includes four categories and label each row with the name and picture of the shape. From this day on, follow the Daily Routine, having children record their contributions as they bring them in.

For Throughout the Month

Analyze Data Discuss the Graph and any changes in it once or twice a week. Some questions that encourage children to observe and analyze the Graph might include the following.

- What do we know about our collection of containers by looking at our Graph?

- How many containers have been brought in so far?

- Can someone tell us how you get your answer?

- What shape do we have the most of now?

- What shape do we have the least of in our collection?

- How many more ___ than ___ do we have?

- How many ___ and ___ do we have together?

HELPFUL HINTS

- The sample note to parents can be adapted to fit your needs.

- Since May and June bring warmer temperatures, it might be fun to have children use the container collection to explore capacity using water. With a permanent marker and tape, label the containers with the letters A, B, C, and so on. Allow children time to select two containers they think will hold the same amount of water if filled to the top. Have the children fill one container with water and then pour water from the first container into the second. It might be helpful for children to use a funnel.

Dear Parents:

We've been learning to recognize and describe the following geometric shapes in class this month:

- cylinders (can shapes)
- rectangular boxes
- cubes

Please encourage your child to point out containers in your home that can be classified as cylinders, rectangular boxes, and cubes. The children have been asked to look at household items headed for the garbage or recycling in order to find and bring to class one clean, discarded container that is one of these shapes. It will be added to the class collection. Your child may bring in one odd-shaped container as well.

Thanks for your support with this project. Please do not send anything made of glass or anything you need returned.

Sincerely,

BIBLIOGRAPHY

Assessment Alternatives in Mathematics: An overview of assessment techniques that promote learning. Berkeley, CA: Regents, University of California, 1989.

Baratta–Lorton, Mary. "The Opening," *Math Their Way Newsletter* 1977–78. Saratoga, CA: The Center for Innovation in Education.

Baratta–Lorton, Mary. *Mathematics Their Way.* Dale Seymour Publications, 1995.

Baratta–Lorton, Mary. *Workjobs II.* Pearson Learning, 1987.

Burk, Donna, Allyn Snider, and Paula Symonds. "The Calendar," *Box It or Bag It.* Salem, OR: Math Learning Center, 1988.

Burns, Marilyn, and Kathy Richardson. "Making Sense out of Word Problems," *Learning.* January, 1981.

Curriculum Development Associates, Inc. *Making Friends with Numbers.* Washington, DC: Curriculum Development Associates, Inc., 1979.

Hoban, Tana. *Is It Red? Is It Yellow? Is It Blue?* New York: Morrow, 1987.

Hoban, Tana. *Is It Rough? Is It Smooth? Is It Shiny?* New York: Greenwillow, 1984.

Kamii, Constance. *Young Children Reinvent Arithmetic: Implications of Piaget's Theory.* New York: Teachers College Press, 1985.

Kanter, Patsy. *Helping Your Child Learn Math.* U.S. Department of Education, 1992.

Marolda, Maria. *Attribute Games and Activities.* Mountain View, CA: Creative Publications, 1997.

National Council of Teachers of Mathematics. *Curriculum and Evaluation Standards for School Mathematics.* Reston, VA: The National Council of Teachers of Mathematics, 1989.

National Council of Teachers of Mathematics. *Mathematics Assessment: Myths, Models, Good Questions and Practical Suggestions.* Reston, VA: The National Council of Teachers of Mathematics, 1991.

Parker, Tom. *In One Day: The Things Americans Do in a Day.* Boston, MA: Houghton–Mifflin, 1984.

Richardson, Kathy. *Developing Number Concepts Using Unifix Cubes.* Reading, MA: Addison–Wesley, 1984.

Wirtz, Robert. *Banking on Problem Solving* and *Think, Talk, Connect.* Washington, DC: Curriculum Development Assoc., Inc., 1980.

Wirtz, Robert. *Drill and Practice at a Problem–Solving Level.* Washington, DC: Curriculum Development Assoc., Inc., 1976.

To the Teacher:

The Assessment component of *Every Day Counts® Calendar Math* includes four tests: Pretest, Winter Test, Spring Test, and Post Test. This arrangement enables you to monitor student progress at significant times during the year. Each test includes an answer key and an accompanying list of tested skills.

The Pretest and Post Test are parallel tests, measuring skills for the whole year. They include questions in various standardized-test formats, including short answer, multiple choice, and in the upper grades, extended response questions.

The Winter and Spring Tests are structured similarly. The Winter Test focuses on skills presented in September, October, and November, and might be given in December or January. The Spring Test covers skills taught in December, January, and February, and might be given in March or April.

Any of these tests will be useful as practice at various times during the year before students take regular standardized tests. They can also be given in shorter form—a page or a few questions at a time.

Following each test is an answer key that includes a list of tested skills, the corresponding test item numbers, and a list of Calendar Math Elements where the skills are presented. This allows you to find places within the program where individual skills can be reinforced in a variety of contexts.

The tests are cumulative in nature, testing skills in ways similar to the way they are taught in Calendar Math, but in slightly different contexts. Students should be able to apply the skills they have learned and experienced in a variety of situations.

Kindergarten teachers:

For each test, give a copy of the test page(s) to children. Write the child's name at the top of each page, or have the child write his or her name. Read the questions aloud and have children mark their answers on the page. Use the locator art to help children find the right page and follow along from question to question. You may want to administer these tests to small groups of 3 or 4 children at a time, or to individuals one-on-one. You may also choose to administer only one page of the test each day.

Read each item aloud.
(Have children look at Pretest page 1.)

1. Put your finger on the star. Look at the hearts in the box. How many hearts are there? Loop the number that tells how many hearts.

2. Put your finger on the ball. Look at the numbers in the circles. What number comes next? Write the number in the empty circle.

3. Put your finger on the house. Look at the numbers in the squares. What number is missing? Write the number in the empty square.

4. Put your finger on the truck. Look at the sneakers. Each sneaker needs a sock. Which group has exactly one sock for each sneaker? Loop the group of socks.

5. Put your finger on the moon. Look at the shapes. Which shape is round on both ends? Draw a loop around the shape.

(Have children turn to the next page.)

6. Put your finger on the apple. Look at the coins. Which one is a nickel? Loop the nickel.

7. Put your finger on the dog. Look at the dominoes. Which domino has a total of 7 dots? Loop the domino with 7 dots.

8. Put your finger on the car. Look at the animals waiting in line. Which animal is third in line? Loop the third animal.

9. Put your finger on the teddy bear. Look at the pattern of shapes. What shape comes next? Draw the shape that comes next.

10. Put your finger on the sun. Look at the flowers. There are 10 flowers in each bunch and some left over. How many flowers are there in all? Loop the number.

(Have children turn to the next page.)

11. Put your finger on the star. Look at the picture of birds. Which number is less than the number of birds in the picture? Loop the number that is less.

12. Put your finger on the ball. Look at the pencil and the paper clip. About how many paper clips long is the pencil? Write the number on the line.

13. Put your finger on the house. Look at the pictures of four different containers. Josie drank a cup of lemonade. Which container holds less than a cup of lemonade?

14. Put your finger on the truck. Rita found a bird's nest with 3 eggs. Then she found another nest with 2 eggs. How many eggs did she find in all? Loop the number.

15. Put your finger on the moon. Look at the picture graph. It shows children's favorite foods: pizza, hot dog, and peanut butter sandwich. How many children like pizza best? Write the number on the line.

NAME _____

1.

   3   4   5   6

2.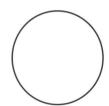

(6)   (7)   (8)   (   )

3.

| 23 | 24 | | 26 |

4.

5.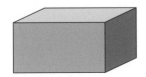

6.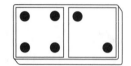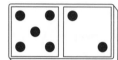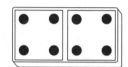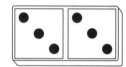

7.

8.

9.

 _____

10.

4   12   22   24

11.

 3 4 5 6

12.

_____
- - - - - - - - -
_____

13.

14.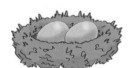

 3 5 6 7

15.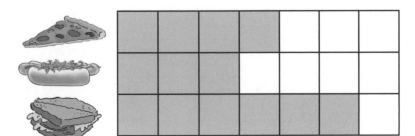

_____
- - - - - - - - -
_____

1. 5

2. 9

3. 25

4. 3rd picture (4 socks)

5. 4th picture (cylinder)

6. 2nd picture (nickel)

7. 2nd picture (4 + 3 = 7)

8. 3rd picture (horse)

9.

☐

10. 22

11. 3

12. 5

13. 4th picture (teaspoon)

14. 5

15. 4

Tested Skills	Item Numbers	Every Day Counts Element(s)
Quantities and numerals	1, 11	Daily Depositor, Domino Number Builder
Counting and sequencing numbers	2, 3	Calendar, Counting Tape and Clip Collection, Daily Depositor
One-to-one correspondence	4	Counting Tape and Clip Collection, Domino Number Builder, Graph
Solid figures and their attributes	5	Calendar
Money	6	Depositor
Grouping and counting by ones, fives, tens	7, 10	Counting Tape and Clip Collection, Daily Depositor
Position words	8	Domino Number Builder
Patterns	9	Calendar
Measuring and comparing	12, 13	Estimation and Measurement, Graph
Solving problems	14	Calendar, Counting Tape and Clip Collection, Domino Number Builder
Interpreting graphs	15	Graph

Read each item aloud.
(Have children look at Winter Test page 1.)

1. Put your finger on the star. Look at the numbers in the circles. What number comes next? Write the number in the empty circle.

2. Put your finger on the ball. Look at the numbers in the squares. What number is missing? Write the number in the empty square.

3. Put your finger on the house. Look at the dots. How many dots are there? Loop the number that tells how many dots.

4. Put your finger on the truck. Look at the groups of juice boxes. Which group has six juice boxes? Loop the group of six.

5. Put your finger on the moon. Look at the cars waiting in line. Which car is second in line? Loop the second car.

(Have children turn to the next page.)

6. Put your finger on the apple. Look at the pattern of shapes. What shape comes next? Draw the shape that comes next.

7. Put your finger on the dog. Look at the row of boxes with dots in them. How many more dots do you need to fill the boxes? Loop the number that tells how many more dots you need.

8. Put your finger on the car. Look at the dominoes. Which domino has a total of five dots? Loop the domino with five dots.

9. Put your finger on the teddy bear. Look at the crayons. The box holds 10 crayons. How many crayons are there in all? Loop the number of crayons.

10. Put your finger on the sun. Jesse is counting by fives. Look at the numbers: 5, 10, 15, 20 . . . What comes next? Loop the number that comes next.

(Have children turn to the next page.)

11. Put your finger on the star. Look at the crayon. Which crayon is longest? Color in the longest crayon.

12. Put your finger on the ball. Look at the pails. Each pail needs a shovel. Which group of shovels has exactly one shovel for each pail? Loop the group of shovels.

13. Put your finger on the house. Look at the pictures: sweater, jacket, gloves, sandals. Which one do you wear when the weather is hot?

14. Put your finger on the truck. Listen to this story. One day, three frogs jumped up on a rock. Then one more frog jumped up on the rock. How many frogs jumped on the rock all together? Loop the number of frogs.

15. Put your finger on the moon. Look at the picture graph. It shows children's favorite zoo animals. How many children like tigers best? Loop the number that tells how many like tigers best.

1.

(1) (2) (3) ( )

2.

| 15 | 16 | | 18 |

3.

   3   4   5   6

4.

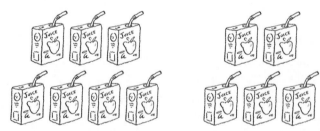 

5.

Name _____

6.  ____

7.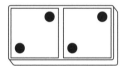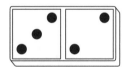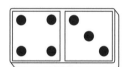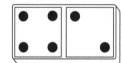

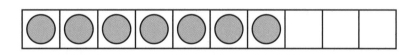

2   1   3   4

8.

9.

4   10   13   14

10.

5, 10, 15, 20, ____

15   21   25   30

11.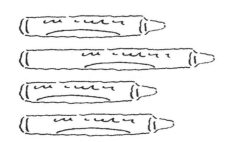

12.

13.

14. 2   3   4   5

15.

2   3

4   5

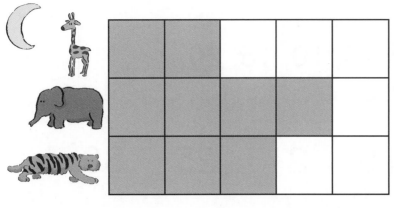

1. 4

2. 17

3. 5

4. 4th picture (6 boxes)

5. 2nd picture

6.

7. 3

8. 2nd picture

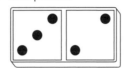

9. 13

10. 25

11. Longest crayon (2nd from top) should be colored in.

12. 2nd picture (4 shovels)

13. 4th picture (sandals)

14. 4

15. 3

Tested Skills	Item Numbers	Every Day Counts Element(s)
Counting and sequencing numbers	1, 2	Calendar, Counting Tape and Clip Collection, Daily Depositor
Quantities and numerals	3, 4	Daily Depositor, Domino Number Builder
Position words	5	Domino Number Builder
Patterns	6	Calendar
Addition and subtraction concepts	7	Counting Tape and Clip Collection, Daily Depositor, Graph
Grouping and counting by ones, fives, tens	8, 9, 10	Counting Tape and Clip Collection, Daily Depositor
Measuring and comparing: length	11	Estimation and Measurement
One-to-one correspondence	12	Counting Tape and Clip Collection, Domino Number Builder, Graph
Temperature	13	Estimation and Measurement, Graph
Solving problems	14	Calendar, Counting Tape and Clip Collection, Domino Number Builder
Interpreting graphs	15	Graph

Read each item aloud.
(Have children look at Spring Test page 1.)

1. Put your finger on the star. Look at the numbers in the circles. What number comes next? Write the number in the empty circle.

2. Put your finger on the ball. Look at the numbers in the squares. What number is missing? Write the number in the empty square.

3. Put your finger on the house. Look at the dots on the domino. Which number means one more than the number of dots on the domino? Loop the number.

4. Put your finger on the apple. Look at the pattern of shapes. Which shape comes next? Draw the shape that comes next.

5. Put your finger on the dog. Look at the shapes. Which one is a triangle? Loop the triangle.

(Have children turn to the next page.)

6. Put your finger on the truck. Look at shapes of the objects. Which shape is a cube? Loop the picture that shows a cube.

7. Put your finger on the teddy bear. Look at the rows of shapes. Which row is the top row? Color in all the shapes in the top row.

8. Put your finger on the car. Look at the squirrels. Each squirrel needs an acorn. Which group of acorns has exactly one acorn for each squirrel? Loop the group of acorns.

9. Put your finger on the moon. Look at the different containers; teaspoon, milk jug, juice box, and paper cup. Which container holds the most? Loop the container that holds the most.

10. Put your finger on the sun. Look at the pictures: cat, mouse, butterfly, horse. Manny has a cat. Which picture shows something that weighs more than a cat? Loop the picture.

(Have children turn to the next page.)

11. Put your finger on the star. Look at the earthworm and the paper clip. About how many paper clips long is the worm? Write the number on the line.

12. Put your finger on the ball. Look at the coins. Which one is a penny? Loop the penny.

13. Put your finger on the house. Paula saw 4 flowers blooming in the garden. Then she saw 3 more flowers. How many flowers did she see all together? Loop the number.

14. Put your finger on the truck. Look at the tally marks. Naureen saw 6 birds at her bird feeder one day. She made a tally mark for each bird. Which picture shows 6 tally marks? Loop the picture.

15. Put your finger on the moon. Look at the picture graph. It shows children's favorite sports. How many children like soccer best? Write the number who like soccer best.

1. 　 **9** 　 **8** 　 **7** 　 ◯

2.  　 **21** 　 **22** 　 ▢ 　 **24**

3. 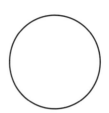 　  　 9 　 10 　 11 　 12

4.

▢ ▢ ▧ ▧ ▢ ▢ ▧ ▧ ▢ _____

5.

6.

7.

○ ○ ○ ○ ○

☐ ☐ ☐ ☐ ☐

▭ ▭ ▭ ▭ ▭

8.

9.

10.

11.

_____

- - - - - - - -

_____

12.

13.

6   7   8   9

14.

////| //// //// ////| ///

15.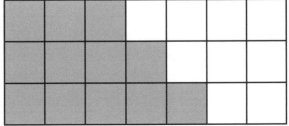

_____

- - - - - - - -

_____

1. 6

2. 23

3. 11

4.

☐

5. 2nd picture (triangle)

6. 2nd picture (dot cube)

7. Top row (circles) should be colored in.

8. 3rd picture (4 acorns)

9. 2nd picture (gallon of milk)

10. 4th picture (horse)

11. 3

12. 4th picture (penny)

13. 7

14. 1st picture (6 tally marks)

15. 5

Tested Skills	Item Numbers	Every Day Counts Element(s)
Counting and sequencing numbers	1, 2	Calendar, Counting Tape and Clip Collection, Daily Depositor
Quantities and numerals	3	Daily Depositor, Domino Number Builder
Patterns	4	Calendar
Triangles	5	Calendar
Three-dimensional shapes	6	Calendar
Position words	7	Domino Number Builder
One-to-one correspondence	8	Counting Tape and Clip Collection, Domino Number Builder, Graph
Measuring and comparing: capacity, weight, length	9, 10, 11	Estimation and Measurement
Money	12	Daily Depositor
Solving problems	13	Calendar, Counting Tape and Clip Collection, Domino Number Builder
Recording data and interpreting graphs	14, 15	Graph

Read each item aloud.
(Have children look at Post Test page 1.)

1. Put your finger on the star. Look at the apples in the basket. How many apples are there? Loop the number that tells how many apples.

2. Put your finger on the ball. Look at the numbers in the circles. What number comes next? Write the number in the empty circle.

3. Put your finger on the house. Look at the numbers in the squares. What number is missing? Write the number in the empty square.

4. Put your finger on the truck. Look at the bowls. Each bowl needs a spoon. Which group has exactly one spoon for each bowl? Loop the group of spoons.

5. Put your finger on the moon. Look at the shapes. Which shape has a square on every side? Draw a loop around the shape.

(Have children turn to the next page.)

6. Put your finger on the apple. Look at the coins. Which one is a dime? Loop the dime.

7. Put your finger on the dog. Look at the dominoes. Which domino has a total of 5 dots? Loop the domino with 5 dots.

8. Put your finger on the car. Look at the children waiting in line at the door. Find the second child in line. Loop the second child.

9. Put your finger on the teddy bear. Look at the pattern of shapes. What shape comes next? Draw the shape that comes next in the empty box.

10. Put your finger on the sun. Look at the cookies. There are 10 cookies on each plate and some left over. How many cookies are there in all? Loop the number.

(Have children turn to the next page.)

11. Put your finger on the star. Look at the picture of kittens. Which number is more than the number of kittens in the picture? Loop the number that is more.

12. Put your finger on the ball. Look at the baseball bat and the pencil. About how many pencils long is the bat? Write the number on the line.

13. Put your finger on the house. Look at the pictures of four containers. Carrie's dad made a pitcher of lemonade. Which container holds more than a pitcher of lemonade?

14. Put your finger on the truck. Miguel went to the fair. He saw one clown with 3 balloons. He saw another clown holding 5 balloons. How many balloons did he see all together? Loop the number.

15. Put your finger on the moon. Look at the bar graph. It shows how many dogs, squirrels, and ducks Madison saw at the park. How many squirrels did she see? Write the number on the line.

1.    5   6   7   8

2.    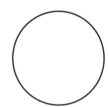 ◯

9   10   11

3. 🏠   19   20   ☐   22

4. 🚚

5. 🌙

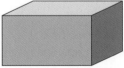

6.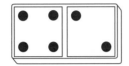

7.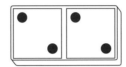

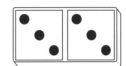 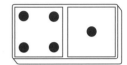

8.

9.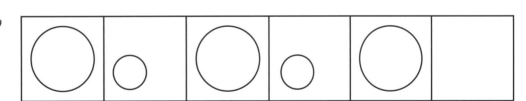

10.

5   32   23   25

11.

3   4   5   6

12.

- - - - - - - -

13.

14.

5   6   7   8

15.

- - - - - - - -

----

1. 6

2. 12

3. 21

4. 1st picture (5 spoons)

5. 3rd picture (cube)

6. 3rd picture (dime)

7. 4th picture (4 + 1 = 5)

8. 2nd child from left

9. (little circle)

10. 23

11. 6

12. 4

13. 1st picture (pail)

14. 8

15. 3

Tested Skills	Item Numbers	Every Day Counts Element(s)
Quantities and numerals	1, 11	Depositor, Domino Number Builder
Counting and sequencing numbers	2, 3	Calendar, Counting Tape and Clip Collection, Depositor
One-to-one correspondence	4	Counting Tape and Clip Collection, Domino Number Builder, Graph
Solid figures and their attributes	5	Calendar
Money	6	Daily Depositor
Grouping and counting by ones, fives, tens	7, 10	Counting Tape and Clip Collection, Daily Depositor
Position words	8	Domino Number Builder
Patterns	9	Calendar
Measuring and comparing	12, 13	Estimation and Measurement, Graph
Solving problems	14	Calendar, Counting Tape and Clip Collection, Domino Number Builder
Interpreting graphs	15	Graph

TEACHING RESOURCES

DAYS OF THE WEEK IN SPANISH

Sunday	domingo
Monday	lunes
Tuesday	martes
Wednesday	miércoles
Thursday	jueves
Friday	viernes
Saturday	sábado

NUMBERS THROUGH 31 IN SPANISH

one	uno
two	dos
three	tres
four	cuatro
five	cinco
six	seis
seven	siete
eight	ocho
nine	nueve
ten	diez
eleven	once
twelve	doce
thirteen	trece
fourteen	catorce
fifteen	quince
sixteen	diez y seis
seventeen	diez y siete
eighteen	diez y ocho
nineteen	diez y nueve
twenty	viente
twenty-one	viente y uno
twenty-two	viente y dos
twenty-three	viente y tres
twenty-four	viente y cuatro
twenty-five	viente y cinco
twenty-six	viente y seis
twenty-seven	viente y siete
twenty-eight	viente y ocho
twenty-nine	viente y nueve
thirty	treinta
thirty-one	treinta y uno

1	2	3	4	5
6	7	8	9	10
11	12	13	14	15
16	17	18	19	20
21	22	23	24	25
26	27	28	29	30
31				

TR1 Date Cards

month _____

Sunday	Monday	Tuesday	Wednesday	Thursday	Friday	Saturday

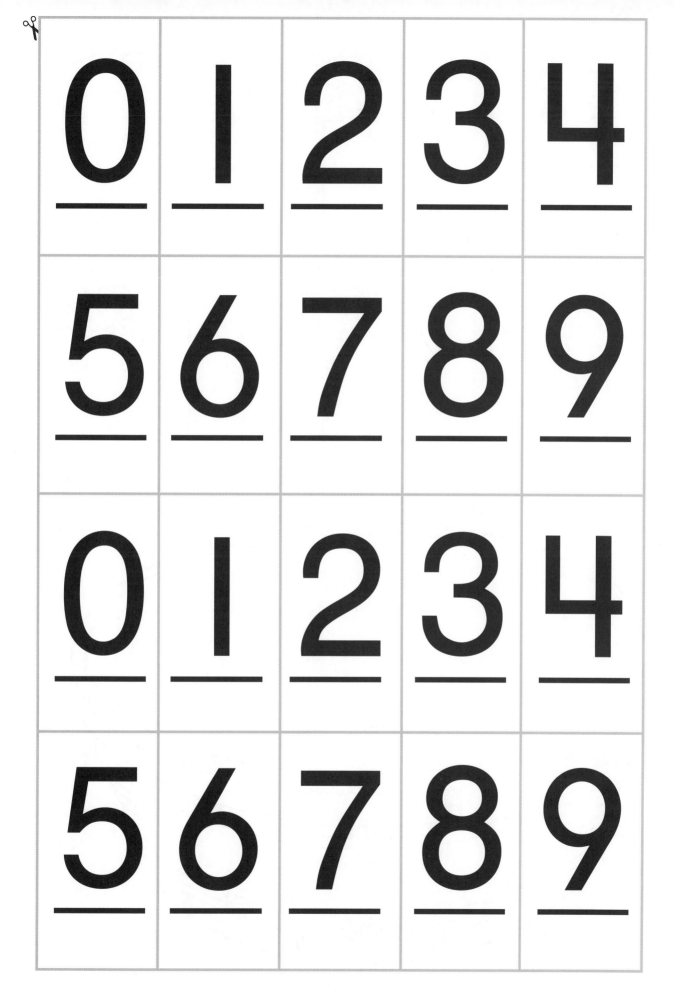

TR3 0–9 Digit Cards

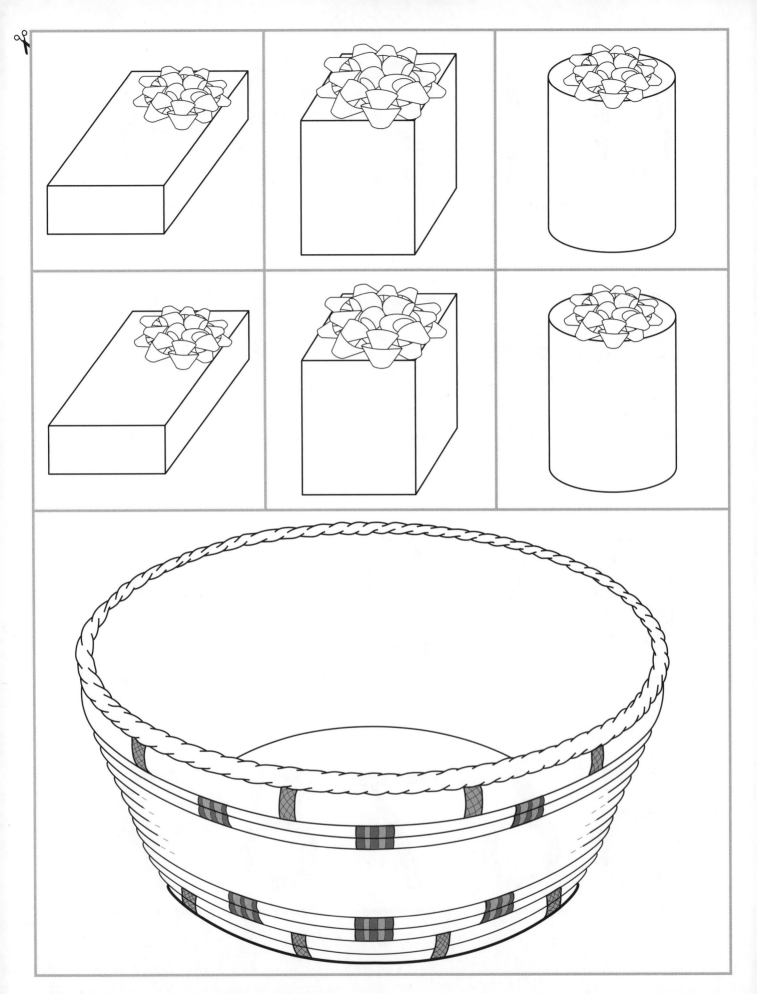

TR4 **Birthday Basket and Present Picture**

TR5 Paper Clip Chains

TR7 Domino Record

TR8 Every Day Graph

TR8 Every Day Graph

TR9 Dotted Domino Halves

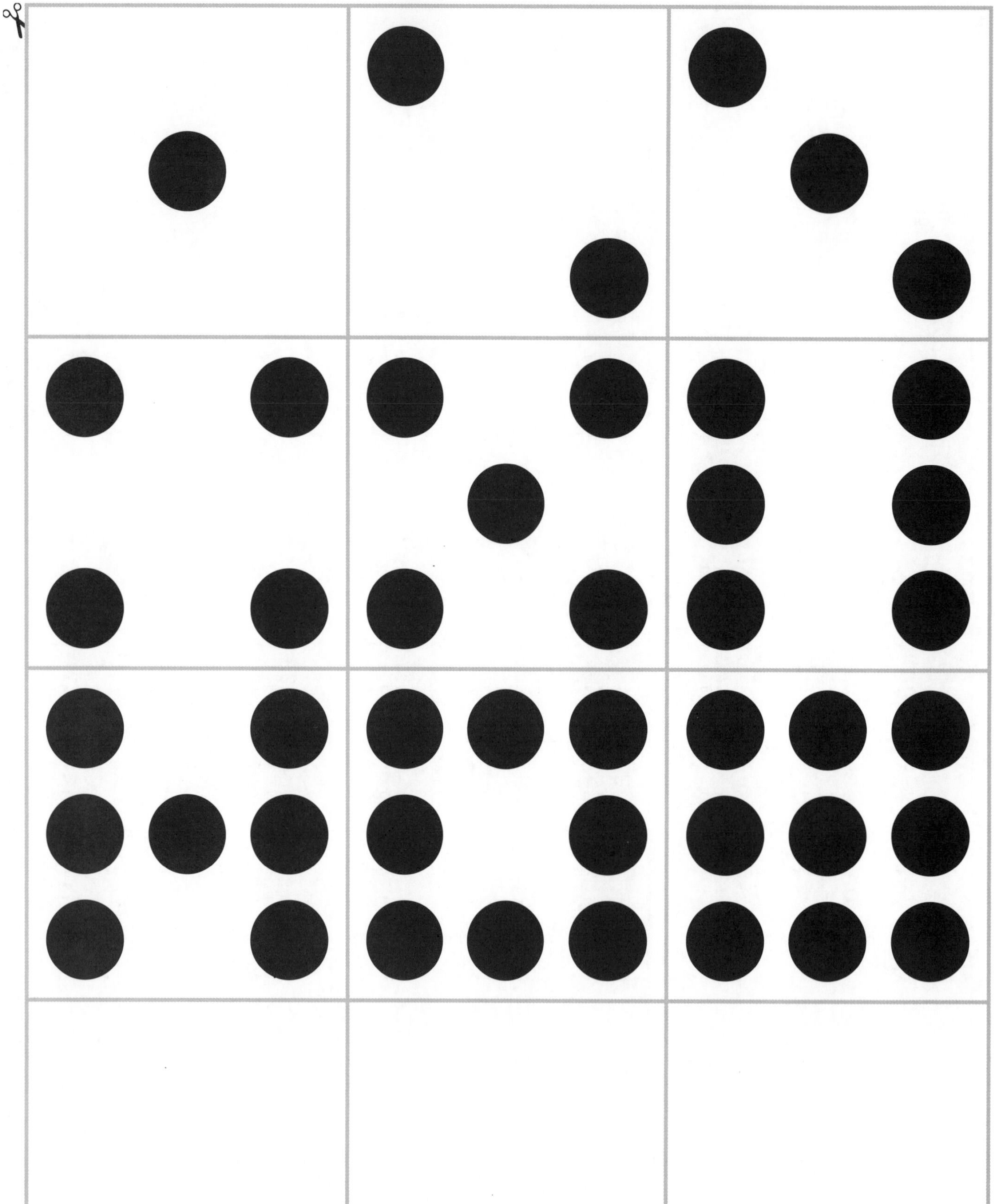

TR10 Domino Halves

TR11 Numeral Dot Cards

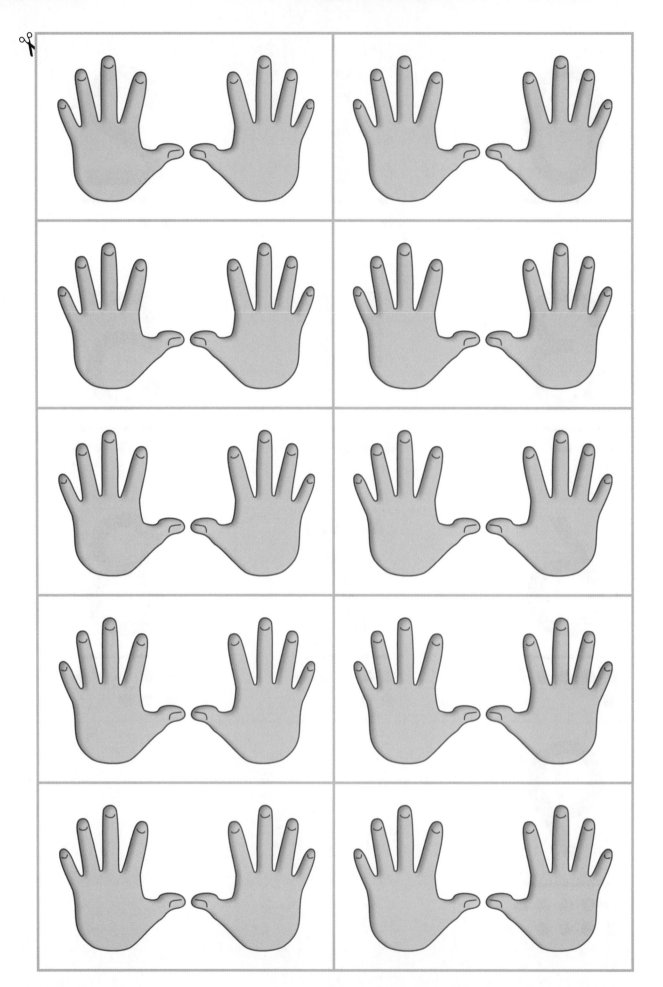

TR12 Paper Hands

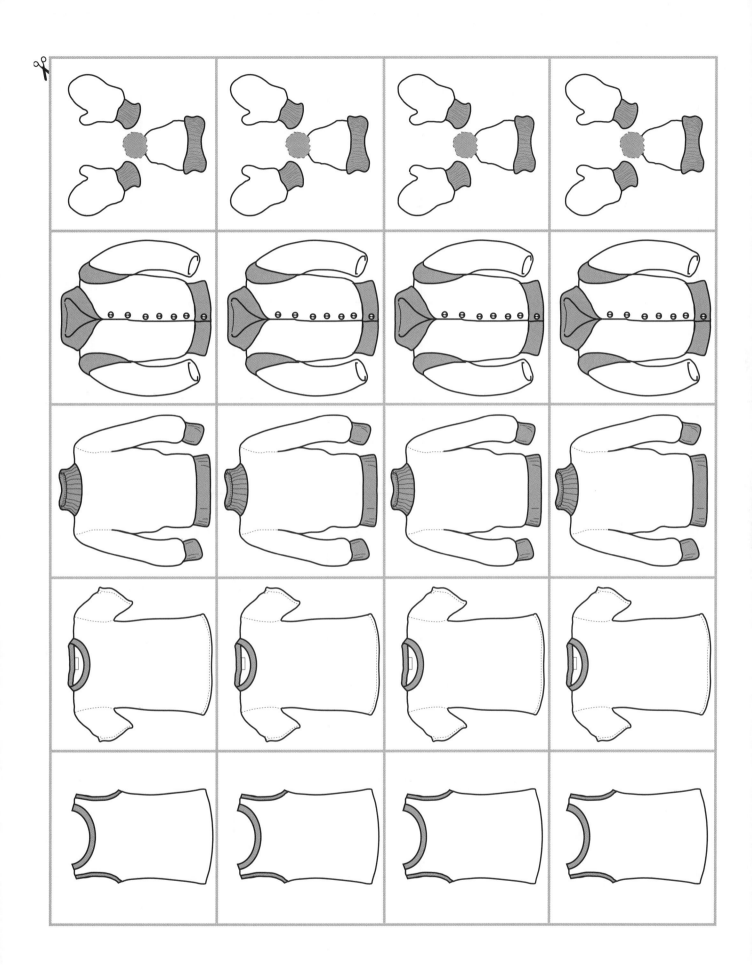

TR13 Clothing Markers

TR15 Double Fives Dotted Dominoes

1 and **1**   **2** and **1**   **3** and **1**

4 and **1**   **5** and **1**   **6** and **1**

7 and **1**   **8** and **1**

TR16 Number Combination Cards ("___ and 1")

$1 + 2$	$2 + 2$	$3 + 2$
$4 + 2$	$5 + 2$	$6 + 2$
$7 + 2$		

1	2	3	4	5	6	7	8	9	10
11	12	13	14	15	16	17	18	19	20
21	22	23	24	25	26	27	28	29	30
31	32	33	34	35	36	37	38	39	40
41	42	43	44	45	46	47	48	49	50
51	52	53	54	55	56	57	58	59	60
61	62	63	64	65	66	67	68	69	70
71	72	73	74	75	76	77	78	79	80
81	82	83	84	85	86	87	88	89	90
91	92	93	94	95	96	97	98	99	100

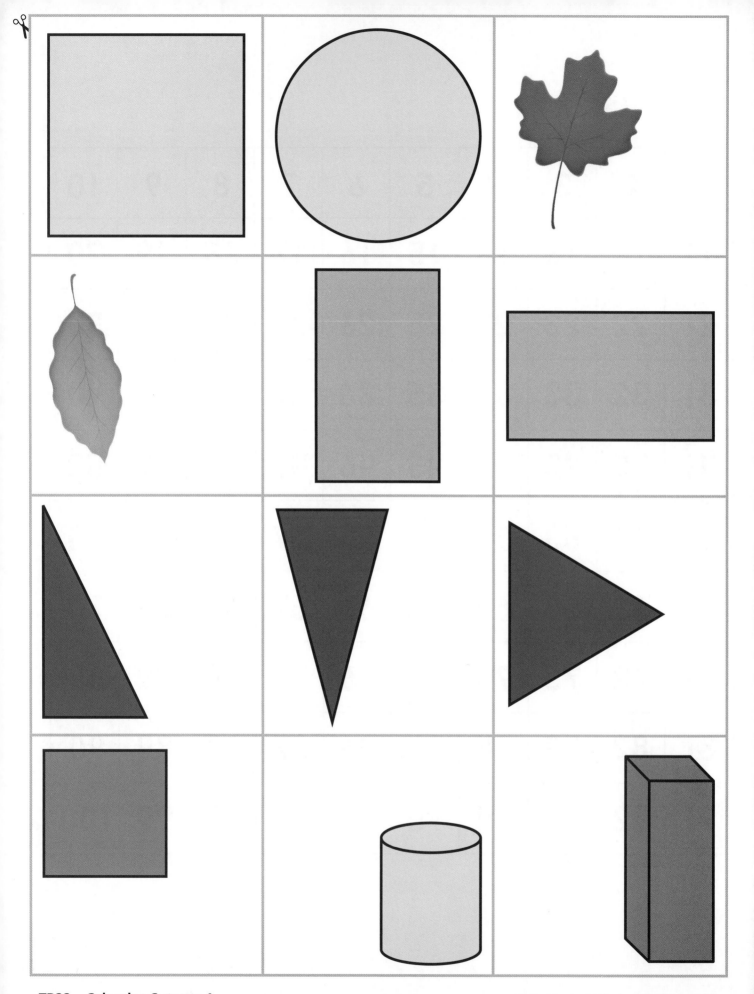

TR22 Calendar Cutouts A

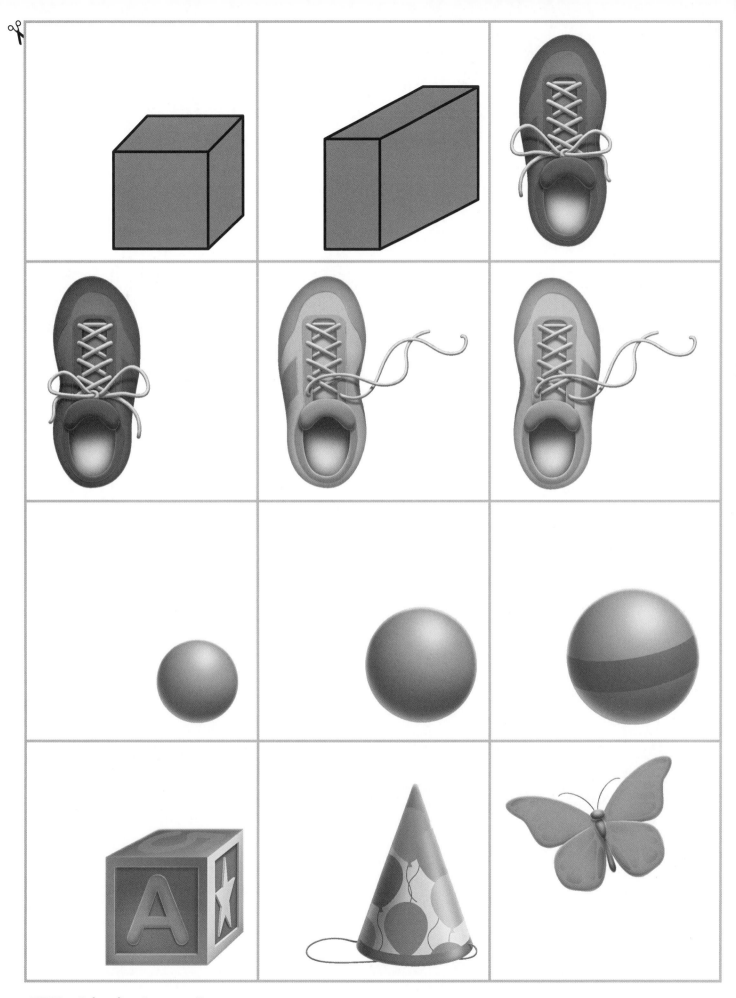

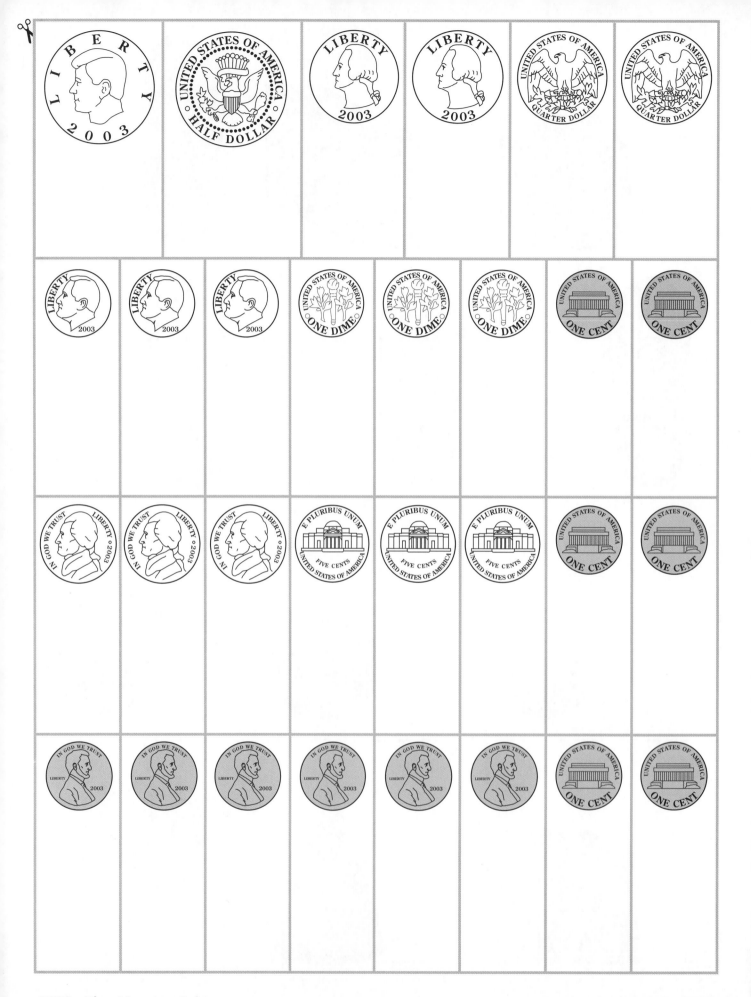

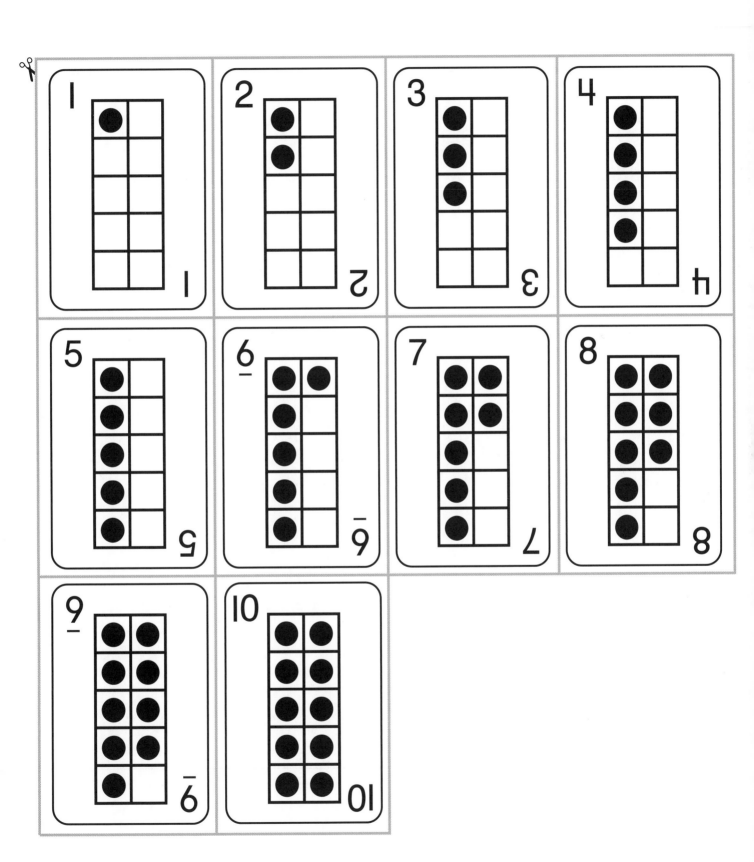

TR25 Ten Grid Number Cards

zero 0	seven 7 :::•••
one 1 •	eight 8 :::••
two 2 ••	nine 9 :::••
three 3 •••	ten 10 :::::
four 4 ••••	penny
five 5 •••••	nickel
six 6 :••••	dime

These might be used to accompany discussions, to build individual student word banks, or to enlarge for a Word Wall.

TR27 Sample Vocabulary A

circle 	sphere 
cylinder 	cone 
rectangle 	square 
rectangular solid 	cube 
triangle 	

These might be used to accompany discussions, to build individual student word banks, or to enlarge for a Word Wall.

TR28 Sample Vocabulary B

INDEX

Addition

addition signs, 105, 120-121

basic facts, 48–49, 64–66, 78–79, 90–91, 105–106, 131–132

concepts, 23, 26, 39–40, 63–66, 88, 90–91, 105–106, 120–121, 131–132

models, 48–49, 64–66, 77–78, 90–91, 105–106, 131–132

number combinations, 64–66, 77–79, 90–91, 105–106, 120–121, 130–131

Algebra

algebraic thinking, 19, 33, 47, 53, 67, 75, 91, 102–103, 108, 117, 120–121

expressions, 41, 65–67, 78–79, 90–91, 105–106, 120–121, 131–132

patterns. *See* Pattern.

Assessment

assessment materials, 137–157

ongoing assessment questions, 18, 21, 24, 27, 32, 34, 39, 41, 46, 48, 50, 52, 54, 56, 60, 62, 64, 66, 67, 70, 74, 75, 77, 79, 80, 82, 87, 90, 92, 94, 98, 102, 103, 105, 106, 108, 112, 116, 118, 120–122, 124, 128, 130–133

Basic facts, 48–49, 64–66, 78–79, 90–91, 105–106, 131–132

Benchmarks. *See* Counting.

Calendar, 18–20, 32–33, 46–47, 60–61, 74–75, 87–88, 102–103, 116–117, 128–129

Capacity, 67–69, 82–83, 108, 120–121, 124–125, 135

Communication

dialogue questions, 18, 21, 24, 27, 32, 34, 37, 39, 41, 46, 48, 50, 52, 54, 56, 60, 62, 64, 66, 67, 70, 74, 75, 77, 79–80, 82, 87, 90, 92, 94, 98, 102, 103, 105, 106, 108, 112, 116, 120–122, 124, 128, 130–133

Comparison

alike/different, 19, 36, 46–47

compare attributes. *See* Capacity, Length, and Weight.

compare quantities, 27–29, 33–43, 50–52, 54–55, 67–71, 75–77, 80–81, 88, 90–97, 106–108, 117, 120–121, 124–125, 130–135

lesser/greater, 23, 53, 60, 82–83, 123

more/fewer/same, 21, 23, 53, 60–61, 65–67, 69, 81–83, 110–111, 116, 125

Counting

by fives, 48–49, 77, 89–91, 111, 130–132

by ones, 18–26, 34–36, 66–67, 75–80, 89–90, 106–108, 120–121

by tens, 34–36, 40, 23–26, 34–36, 50–51, 62–64, 77, 89–90, 103–104, 106–108, 112–113, 118–119, 120–121, 124–125, 132–133

concrete objects, 23–26, 34–36, 50–53, 80–81, 90–91, 94–97, 133–135

counting back, 21–26, 40, 46–47, 60–61, 66–67, 74–75, 79–80, 87–88, 90–94, 104, 106–108, 120–122, 132–133

counting on, 20–26, 32–34, 40, 46–47, 52–53, 60–61, 64, 66–67, 87–88, 90–94, 104, 106–108, 118–122, 130–133

grouping

  by fives, 48–49, 77, 89–91, 111, 130–132

  by tens, 24–26, 34–36, 39–41, 48–49, 52–53, 66–67, 69, 75–77, 79–80, 89–90, 92–94, 103–104, 112–113, 124–125, 130

  by twos, 90–94

one–to–one correspondence, 18–26, 34–41, 46–49, 50–52, 55, 62–66, 74–75, 77–79, 89–94, 103–104, 124–125, 132–133

using 5 and 10 as benchmarks, 23, 35, 40–41, 48–49, 62–64, 110, 118–119, 124–125

Days of the week. *See* Time.

Data analysis. *See also* Graphing.

analyzing data, 28, 55, 67–71, 81, 88, 94–97, 108–111, 122–123, 133–134

collecting/recording data, 27–29, 41–43, 54–57, 67–71, 80–83, 94–97, 108–111, 122–123, 133–134

making predictions, 70–71, 81, 94–97, 108–111, 113, 120, 122–123, 131, 133–134

tables, 57, 81–82, 96, 110–111, 113, 131

tally marks, 81–83, 89–90

Estimation

measurement, 22, 56–57, 69–71, 82–83, 98–99, 112–113, 124–125

strategies, 23, 56–57, 69–71, 82–83, 98–99, 124–125

Evaluation. *See* Assessment.

Fractions

concepts, 87–88, 117, 124–125

one–half, 87–88, 117

Geometry

corner, 28–29, 60–61, 116–117, 134

face, 28–29, 75, 116–117, 134

plane shapes. *See* Plane shapes.

properties of plane shapes, 46–47, 60–61

properties of solids, 29, 102–103, 116–117, 133–135

relate 3–dimensions to 2–dimensions, 27–29, 56–58, 60–62, 67–69, 74–75, 102–103, 116–117, 133–135

relationships between plane shapes, 56–58, 60–61

side, 28–29, 47, 60–61, 75, 96, 109, 116–117, 134

solid figures. *See* Solids.

Graphing

bar graph, 41–43, 67–69, 80–81

create a graph, 27–29, 41–43, 67–69, 80–81, 122–123, 133–135

interpret a graph, 27–29, 41–43, 80–81, 122–123, 133–135

picture graph, 27–29, 54–55, 67–69, 80–81, 122–123, 133–135

Home involvement, 62, 64, 67, 80, 86, 97, 111, 135

Hundreds, 24, 80, 86, 92–94, 106–108, 121–122, 132–133

Hundredth Day, 24, 80, 86

Length

height (taller/shorter), 52, 57, 71, 83, 124–125

length (shorter/longer), 43, 56–57, 64, 98–99

Literature,

bibliography, 136

Manipulatives

classroom objects, 34, 37, 41, 47, 52, 56–57, 62, 70–71, 82–83, 98–99

real–world objects, 27–29, 34–36, 41, 48–49, 67–69, 80, 112–113, 124–125, 134–135

Measurement

capacity. *See* Capacity.

estimating, 56–57, 82–83, 98–99, 112–113, 124–125

length. *See* Length.

measurement comparisons,

   between/middle, 94, 102–103

   big/bigger/biggest, 36, 102–103

   heavy/heavier/heaviest, 69–71

   large/larger/largest, 102–103

   little/littler/littlest, 102–103

   long/longer/longest, 43, 56–57, 64, 98–99

   short/shorter/shortest, 43, 56–57, 64, 98–99

   small/smaller/smallest, 56–57

nonstandard units, 56–57, 67–69, 70–71, 82–83

ordering, 56–57, 67–69, 70–71

pan balance, 69 –71

perimeter, 24

temperature. *See* Temperature.

time. *See* Time.

volume. *See* Volume.

weight. *See* Weight.

Mental math, 20–24, 32–34, 39–41, 46–47, 52–53, 66–67, 74–75, 77–80, 92–94, 106–108, 120–121, 132–133

Models. *See* Manipulatives.

Music

songs/chants, 19, 24, 28, 60, 74

Money

dime, 118–119, 130–131

nickel, 108–111, 130–131

penny, 94–97, 108–111, 118–119, 130–131

Number

comparing, 21, 23, 28, 32–34, 37, 40, 46–47, 60–61, 66–67, 74–75, 89–94, 105–106, 128–129

instantly recognizing small sets, 37–38, 50–52, 87–88, 90–91, 120–121

matching a numeral to a quantity, 21–26, 34–41, 50–52, 66–67, 75–79, 89–90, 92–94, 103–108, 112–113, 120–121, 124–125, 131–133

number combinations, 64–66, 77–79, 90–91, 105–106, 120–121, 130–131

numeral recognition, 21–24, 32–34, 38, 48–52, 62–67, 75–80, 89–94, 103–108, 118–122, 130–132

ordering, 18–26, 32–34, 39–41, 46–47, 52–53

pattern. *See* Pattern.

reading/writing numerals, 21–24, 32–34, 38, 48–52, 62–67, 75–80, 89–94, 103–108, 118–122, 130–132

Number sense

benchmarks, 24–26, 39–40, 52–53, 66–67, 74–75, 77–78, 92–97, 106–108, 121–122, 132–133

cardinal numbers, 20, 34–37, 48–49, 50–52, 62–64, 75–79, 89–90, 103–104, 118–119, 130–132

ordinal numbers, 28, 33, 40, 60–61, 79–80, 102–103, 106, 117

Operations. *See* Addition and Subtraction.

Ordering

by size. *See* Length, Weight, and Capacity

numbers. *See* Number.

Patterns

extending, 20, 46–47, 60–61, 74–75, 87–88, 102–103, 116–117, 128–129

identifying, 20, 23, 32–34, 40, 46–47, 52–53, 60–61, 66–67, 74–75, 79–80, 87–88, 102–103, 116–117, 122–123, 128–129

predicting, 18–20, 32–34, 60–61, 87–88, 102–103, 121–122, 128–129

types of

color, 18–20, 23, 32–34, 46–47, 60–61

growing, 120, 128–129

repeating, 18–21, 23, 32–34, 46–47, 60–62, 74–75, 87–90, 102–103, 116–117, 128–129

number, 21–24, 37–38, 40, 64–66, 77–78, 92–94, 106–108, 121–122

shape, 32–34, 60–61

Place value

models, 23, 24–26, 39–40, 50–53, 62–63, 67, 75–77, 80, 89–90, 93, 103–104, 107, 118–119, 122, 130, 133

regrouping, 24–26, 39–40, 50–53, 62–63, 67, 75–77, 80, 89–90, 93, 103–104, 107, 118–119, 122, 130, 133

Plane shapes

circles, 18–20, 29, 46–47, 133–135

rectangles, 29, 46–47, 133–135

squares (square rectangles), 22–23, 29, 46–47, 60–61, 133–135

triangles, 60–61

Polygons. *See* Plane shapes.

Positional words, 21, 23, 32–34, 40, 61, 66–67, 77–79, 92, 112, 134

Probability

exploring likelihood, 94–97, 108–111

organizing results of experiments, 94–97, 108–111

performing simple experiments, 94–97, 108–111

predicting outcomes, 94–97, 108–111, 122

Problem solving

acting it out, 22, 32–34, 47, 62, 111–113, 119, 128

compare strategies, 23, 64, 77

finding a pattern, 28, 47, 53, 61, 77, 80, 91, 131–132

guess and check, 51, 53, 61,112–113

logical reasoning, 51, 80, 91, 131–132

number stories, 38, 50–52, 65–66, 91, 106, 120–121

spatial problem solving, 28, 34, 47, 50–52, 62, 77–79, 131–132

Quantities. *See* Comparison.

Reasoning

logical, 51, 53, 80, 91, 131–132

observing patterns, 19–21, 23, 47, 53, 61, 67, 75, 82–83, 88, 91, 93, 102–103, 111, 122, 131–132

recognizing relevant information, 28, 47, 67, 131

Rectangles. *See* Plane shapes.

Reflections (flips), 29, 87–88

Rotations (turns), 29, 46–47

Shapes. *See* Plane shapes *and* Solids.